Creative Survival in Educational Bureaucracies

Dale L. Brubaker
Roland H. Nelson, Jr.

University of North Carolina at Greensboro

McCutchan Publishing Corporation
2526 Grove Street
Berkeley, California 94704

Library of Congress Catalog Card Number 73-17608

International Standard Book Number 0-8211-0125-0

ABOUT THE AUTHORS

Dale L. Brubaker has had a variety of educational experiences as a public school teacher and university professor. He has been a professor at the University of California, Santa Barbara, the University of Wisconsin, Milwaukee, and the University of North Carolina, Greensboro, where he is presently located. He is the author and co-author of several books that focus on the teacher as a decision-maker in the schools.

Roland H. Nelson, Jr., has spent twenty years as an educational administrator. He served as public school principal, private school headmaster, department chairman, and university dean. He also served as President of Richmond Professional Institute, Provost of Virginia Commonwealth University, and President of Marshall University. He is currently Professor of Educational Administration at the University of North Carolina, Greensboro.

Foreword

Fed on a diet of such books as *How Children Fail, Death at an Early Age,* and *Thirty-Six Children,* many preservice and inservice teachers have struggled with the dilemma of introducing programs that enhance individualistic, creative, and humanistic attributes in youth. These people enrolled in teacher education programs and quickly attached themselves to resident gurus who reinforced their nascent theology with revelations about individualized learning, open classrooms, and affective domains, made manifest through appropriate media, strategies of teaching, and environments for learning. Bearing their standards they went forth into the infidel world, confident in their cause and certain that their ranks would soon swell with converts and upcoming generations of new crusaders.

What they had not counted on, what their gurus had largely neglected, was the real world of the school, the milieu in which it exists and the agonizing slowness with which change takes place. Nor had they adequately realized that their battle was to be a personal and individual one against a highly institutionalized organization, controlled and sanctioned de jure by state and federal laws and de facto by the attitudes, values, and norms of the local citizenry and school bureaucrats.

Can such dissipation of talent be avoided? Dale Brubaker and Roland Nelson believe so—by helping teachers discover the authority and influence patterns that exist in their schools and by helping them establish the values, attitudes, and skills necessary to function as decision-makers. This is the essence of their book.

An effective decision-maker has many important characteristics. He knows his school milieu intimately and recognizes that it is a sociopolitical system with basic functions to perform and for which it is held accountable. He realizes that the school is necessarily organized bureaucratically to perform its functions and to anticipate and deal with public reaction. He has also worked out with the bureaucracy a large measure of professional (as distinct from bureaucratic) control of just how the school functions are to be performed and how much emphasis to give each one. In short, he has real control over variables related to learning and curriculum: individual and group needs and desires, available resources, rewards and sanctions, group norms, informal influence patterns, and others.

But—and this is crucial—the decision-maker also has to give himself over to discovering what he values and how dearly, and then to relate these to the values supported by his school. Anyone who has tried to do this knows how difficult it is.

This is a tall order for a book this size, but it acquits itself very well. First, it is clearly and simply written, allowing its sound ideas to stand out. It is also internally consistent and logical. Because the authors identify their own values, and often why they hold them, I felt compelled to examine my beliefs, particularly when using the self-inventories. Through these devices and descriptions of real examples, the reader is put into aspects of the decision-making role. I believe that the substantive and procedural structure Brubaker and Nelson provide could have an influence on educational practice far beyond books of more popular acclaim. It will take earnest, analytical work, however, and an accompanying willingness to commit oneself to such tasks as against the more easily achieved and perhaps more popular role of martyr.

John G. Chaltas
University of New Hampshire

Introduction

Organizations, like individuals, have their own personalities, and educational organizations are no exception. Organizations also achieve different maturity levels at different times in their existence. This is another way of saying that organizations, subsystems within them, and individuals who are members of organizations are constantly involved in interaction and change. This view is quite different from many people's stated perceptions of organizations: "You can't beat the establishment." "I'm tired of fighting the bureaucracy." "This is the last chance we have to change the establishment." Such expressions miss the mark, for they assume that all organizations are alike at any given time, and further intimate that the organization being discussed is monolothic, omnipotent, and omniscient.

Creative Survival in Educational Bureaucracies has been written to examine and challenge just such oft-stated generalizations. It is our thesis that the individual as a decision-maker in educational organizations can both creatively survive in and change them, *if* such organizations are clearly understood for what they are at any given time in their development.

The book is designed primarily for three audiences: (1) It is directed toward practitioners in educational organizations—those who make decisions as administrators, curriculum planners, and teachers; (2) it is directed to those who are studying to be practitioners; and (3) it is directed to any who are curious about and would like to know more about what goes on in educational organizations.

This book should help the reader better understand the realities of educational organizations. It should help him perceive the differences between what actually goes on and what the rhetoric of educational institutions would have one believe goes on. Further, it is a guide to changing educational organizations so that they may better achieve what decision-makers in the organizations want to do. We believe that if you wish to change something within an organization, you must first know the organization as it is. There must be comprehension of the base point—the status quo of the organization—before one can begin to change it in any systematic and practical way. Finally, operational guides are presented to enable the reader to increase his chances for success in bringing about the changes he wants.

Many critics of education seem to have given up on schools and colleges as viable institutions. Ivan Illich is possibly the most sweeping in his criticism of the schools, and suggests that our only hope is to "deschool society" [*Deschooling Society* (New York: Harper & Row, 1971)]. Our position is that schools as they now exist are not dead, though some may be seriously ill. Certainly, schools are not as healthy as they should be, but much more can be done within present educational organizations than is now being done if those who work within them (1) truly understand how those organizations work, (2) recognize the realistic limitations of what can be done and avoid a "free-floating change" syndrome, and (3) systematically set out to change those aspects of the school or college according to priorities of what they are most likely to be able to do, combined with priorities of what they most want to do.

The reader will find that we have looked at educational organizations as subsystems within the system of formal education. We contend that although nomenclature, stated goals, and objectives may differ among the subsystems, the basic functions performed and the basic organizational structure for performing them are more similar than dissimilar. This is not a book that all will or should want to read from cover to cover. Several sections stand on their own and can be read selectively by those who are interested in only certain aspects of education. For example, those whose primary interests are in elementary and secondary education might focus on chapters 1, 2, and 3 and on certain operational guides and cases that are pertinent to those guides. Readers most concerned with higher education might focus on chapters 1, 2, and 4, and the operational guides and cases that relate directly to higher education.

We do suggest that each reader recognize that elementary schools, secondary schools, and colleges do not differ as much as they would have us believe they differ. Further, to understand thoroughly what goes on in a high school, one certainly needs more than a cursory acquaintance with what has happened to the students before they got to high school, and what is likely to happen to them if they continue on to college.

Part 1, "A Framework for Understanding Educational Organizations," sets the stage so that the educational decision-maker can make sense out of various practices in grades kindergarten through twelve and in higher education as well. Our rationale for focusing on formal education—kindergarten through higher education—is relatively simple: One's understanding of any one part of formal education is enhanced by understanding its relationship to other parts and to the whole. Both the kindergarten teacher and the university president should understand the flow of formal education.

Chapter 1 is basically concerned with viewing educational organizations as sociopolitical systems, and sets forth some of the elements necessary to understand how decisions are made. The reader is provided with a sociopolitical system model with its various elements, e.g., objectives, norms, rewards and sanctions, and evaluation.

Chapter 2 describes the instructional functions that educational institutions do in fact perform. The five functions that educational organizations perform are identified and described: confinement, training, indoctrination, sorting, and providing the conditions for personal or self-development. Our interest is in how such functions are performed and the degree of emphasis given to each function.

Chapters 3 and 4 discuss elementary and secondary schools and institutions of higher learning, respectively, as bureaucratic organizations, pointing up the weaknesses of bureaucracy as a form of organization for schools if they truly are to do for their students what they claim to do. It is argued in these chapters that the bureaucratic model is appropriate for some functions (governance) but inappropriate for others (curriculum and instruction). We then propose a new model designed to achieve a marriage of the bureaucratic and professional models in educational organizations.

Part 2, "How to Survive in and Change Educational Organizations: Operational Guides to Decision-Making," places the reader squarely in the position of decision-maker. This section of the book is more personal and is directed to the reader with one major purpose in mind: how to survive creatively in educational organizations, and in turn change them. Chapter 5 focuses on certain operational guides to decision-making and offers cases illustrating how those guides can help the practitioner better understand the milieu in which he works. Chapters 6, 7, and 8 contain further sets of guides and appropriate cases. The cases are taken from life; names and places are disguised for obvious reasons, to protect both the "guilty" and the innocent.

Throughout the book there are decision-making activities designed to involve the reader in the decision-making process. As the reader becomes involved, he should formulate his own operational guides and develop his own strategies for bringing about change in his particular educational organization, change that will enable him to do his job as he feels it should be done. He should recognize that within his present organization he can do much more than he may now think he can. He is not at the mercy of those above; he can influence critical policy decisions affecting his work, and not only can he survive in an educational bureaucracy, he can do so creatively, by changing it.

Contents

Part 1

A Framework for Understanding Educational Organizations

Decision-makers in educational organizations need to see what occurs as more than a series of isolated events. It is helpful to see events in a larger perspective or framework that will aid the decision-maker in analyzing, planning, and participating in the work of the organization.

Several frameworks are presently available to the decision-maker to help him see the educational process clearly. One can study educational organizations from the vantage-point of history—the approach that is the basis for history of education classes. A second outlook is primarily philosophical; the more traditional approach is to identify several schools of thought, such as idealism, realism, pragmatism, and reconstructionism, placing particular educators and their ideas in one of these categories. A third approach, the basis for the present chapter, is rooted in the behavioral sciences rather than in the humanities. The framework consists of elements—concepts that are useful in studying the past. The main emphasis of our approach is on planning and participation, the basic aspects of the decision-making process.

We do not claim that the sociopolitical framework we have adopted should be taken at face value by the reader, for we hope the reader will build his own framework. We do, however, believe that the reader can find the sociopolitical framework useful in that it gives him something to react to and in the process make sense out of present educational practices. The reader may wish to skip chapter 1 and move directly to other chapters, after which a reading of chapter 1 will be helpful.

A Self-Inventory of Beliefs on Educational Organizations as Sociopolitical Systems

Name________________________________ Section_____Date_______

We would like you to participate in the following exercise in order for you to see where you stand before reading chapter 1. After you have read chapter 1 and discussed ideas from it, you may wish to go through the exercise once again to see if any changes have occurred in your thinking.

To record your responses to the following statements, write the code on the right side of the page. If you strongly agree with a statement, write SA beside its corresponding number on the sheet; if you agree, write A; if you disagree, write D; and if you strongly disagree, write SD.

(1) History provides us with the best framework for understanding the present nature of educational organizations in the United States. ______

(2) Philosophy provides us with the best framework for understanding the present nature of educational organizations in the United States. ______

(3) The behavioral sciences provide us with the best framework for understanding the present nature of educational organizations in the United States. ______

(4) If the decision-maker employs concepts such as objectives, role, status, rewards and sanctions, and

the like in studying the school as a sociopolitical system, the same concepts will be useful (will transfer) in studying any other organization. ______

(5) Most utterances by man are an attempt to get the party or parties with whom he communicates to agree with such utterances. ______

(6) It is both possible and desirable to state goals and objectives in behavioral terms. ______

(7) Cognitive objectives such as remembering, recalling, thinking, and problem solving need to be emphasized more, and affective objectives that focus on the students' feelings need to be emphasized less. ______

(8) Most lists of educational ends clearly indicate who is expected to reach them.

(9) Formal organizations rely more on authority than influence and informal organizations rely more on influence than authority. ______

(10) The role of chance in decision-making is usually a minor one. ______

(1)

Educational Organizations as Sociopolitical Systems

To be a member of an educational organization is to make decisions continually. The following, for example, are some of the decisions a first-year teacher made in a single day:

(1) She arrived at school early and arranged chairs for small group discussion.

(2) She assigned students to various groups on the basis of reading ability.

(3) She handed out books for different groups.

(4) She sought students' advice about objectives for the unit of study.

(5) She handed out information as to how she would grade the students.

(6) She sent a child to the principal's office for swearing in class.

(7) She handed in attendance forms for the day.

(8) She accepted an appointment to the school's curriculum committee.

(9) She remained for an hour after school talking with students.

(10) She went home determined not to think about school again until the next morning.

In examining these decisions, one is impressed both by their scope and by the demands made on the teacher's energies. We also note that the teacher operated on the basis of a foundation of beliefs as to what should be, what could be, and how she would go about realizing such beliefs. That is, the teacher's value system was reflected in her overall objectives, her political decisions that forced her to compromise between her ideal beliefs and what was in her judgment possible, and more technical decisions designed to implement her beliefs.

If we return to the ten decisions for a second look, we are cognizant not so much of what they tell us but of what they fail to tell us. For example, what kinds of pressures were exerted by students, colleagues, and administrators, and how did such pressures influence the decisions? How did our first-year teacher relate to others in the school, especially students, colleagues, and administrators, but also to parents, members of the community, etc? Why did our first-year teacher make the decisions she made? What were some of her motives? In short, how can we make sense out of her seemingly isolated actions?

It is this question to which we address ourselves in this chapter, for it is our belief that we can make sense out of educational decisions by placing them in an analytical framework. Our framework is simply titled a sociopolitical system, for we are particularly interested in the political dimensions of decision-making within the social context.

Dictionaries define the word *system* to mean "an assemblage of objects united by some form of regular interaction or interdependence; an organic or organized whole, as, the solar system; or a new telegraph system." Our interest, of course, is in man-made systems rather than natural systems. Likewise, we are primarily interested in man's relation to man. Our primary focus in this book is on the school as a sociopolitical system and on ways in which the elements of this system are coordinated or orchestrated in order for it to function.

Before discussing the elements of sociopolitical systems we should note that any system demonstrates continuing tension between two forces: unlimited needs or desires and limited resources (resources include money, facilities, people, and time). The political processes that deal with this tension are the subject of chapters 2–8. It is precisely the job of the formal organization to allocate resources available in a *predictable* manner. Given its objectives, the formal organization tries to develop rational, clear-cut methods to reach its objectives. To coordinate various elements of the system in an efficient manner, the formal organization attempts to control relationships among the various elements of the system.

A second thing to note with regard to sociopolitical systems is the distinction between formal and informal organizations. In a sociopolitical system such as a school or a university, formal organizations represent the formal power structure of the organization and as such have a legitimacy seldom ascribed to informal organizations. Examples of formal organizations are a faculty curriculum committee, the administrative council, and faculty organizations. Informal organizations were thought at one time to be a threat to the more formal structure of organizations, but recent literature indicates a reversal in this kind of thinking.[1] Informal organizations, such as the second hour coffee group (discussed later), are usually less predictable than formal organizations. Often they are formed by chance, in the example of the coffee group by the teaching schedule. As soon as an informal organization becomes more formal through systematic planning of activities, it becomes a formal organization in its own right.[2] A group of tennis players who want to organize a tennis team is an example of this process.

Formal Organizations

In this section we will identify and discuss elements common to all formal organizations, to provide the reader with the conceptual tools necessary for studying the school as a sociopolitical system.

Purposes, Goals, and Objectives

In most of the literature describing formal organizations the terms *purposes, goals,* and *objectives* are used interchangeably. We found it useful to make a distinction among these three terms, so that the reader may better comprehend what services educational organizations are truly providing their students.

Purposes are the overall aims of an organization. The organization can control its purposes only in a limited way, since so many external forces exercise control over those purposes. We have found it useful in looking at purposes to view organizations as living organisms having specific needs not unlike the needs of individuals.

The purposes of an organization can be best understood if the organization is viewed as constantly moving or trying to move from one purpose level to another. Any organization may at one time be performing some functions at one level and others at another level, but it will be operating primarily at one purpose level at one given point in time. We have adopted Maslow's needs hierarchy as a model to explain the purpose hierarchy of organizations.[3] We view organizations as having four maturity levels, each of which will, of course, have many subpurposes relating to it. These levels are, in ascending importance:

Level 1—Survival: the organization's very existence is at stake.

Level 2—Commergence: the organization wants to be known as a "status" institution that belongs with other "status" institutions.

Level 3—Differentiation: secure in belonging, the organization can now differentiate and take some chances.

Level 4—Self-actualization: experimentation and creativity are the norm.

The fact that the organization itself cannot control the purpose level at which it may be operating is a function of the influence and controls exercised by its various clients, e.g., taxpayers, alumni, business interests, governmental agencies. For example, a college might aspire to operate above the survival level, but external exigencies have generated financial problems keeping it there. (A more thorough explanation of this purpose model is found in chapter 4, particularly as it relates to the purpose hierarchy of colleges.) A school district that has consistently lost bond issues at the polls could well be at the survival level, though those within the organization aspire to a higher level. In short, though the organization, school, or college can influence the purpose level at which it is operating, it cannot have complete, or in many cases major, control over it.

Goals are statements of generalized intent. Their abstract nature makes them ideal for public relations statements and for operating guidelines for those who work within an organization. Goal statements are not quantifiable, and hence do not lend themselves to measurement. Since they are so general, there is usually minimal disagreement about goal statements until they are operationalized—more specifically, until given objectives are set forth that are supposed to help meet the stated goals of the organization. Examples of goals are:

Education should provide for the general welfare of students.

Citizens in our society should know that they are entitled to due process of law.

Students should find it enjoyable to attend classes in our university.

Goals enable those within the schools or colleges to have bench marks against which they can judge specific actions. For example, if a school had as a goal, "Education should provide for the general welfare of students," and a teacher consistently treated students in a manner that in the judgment of her colleagues did not provide for the students' general welfare, the goal could be used to bring the teacher to task—specifically, to ask her to justify her actions in terms of the stated goal.

Objectives are specific statements that are quantifiable and objectively stated. Some examples of objectives are:

The student will demonstrate that he has learned the multiplication tables up to twelve by scoring at least 90 percent on a written examination.

The university will enroll 10 percent more students during fall registration.

Objectives should of course contribute to goals, and they should be consistent with each other. One of the problems in working with objectives is that they may become the total focus of the school or college, to the point that those making decisions lose sight of the original goals of the organization. If this happens, external forces may well begin to exert so much pressure that an organization operating at the differentiation stage of maturity may find itself reduced to operating at the commergence stage, or even possibly at the survival stage. This phenomenon of overly focusing on objectives is referred to by many social scientists as "goal displacement."

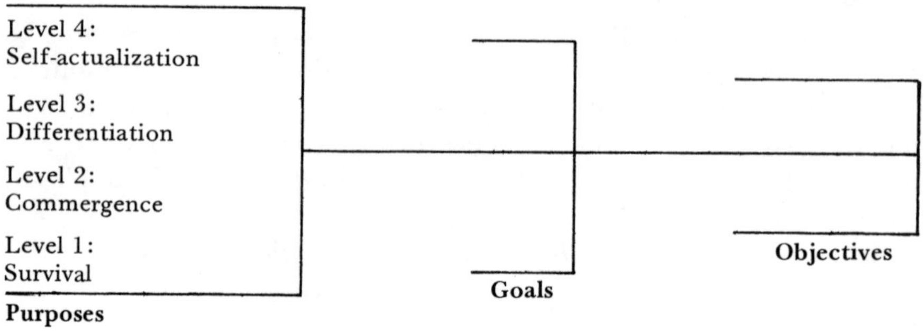

Figure 1:1. Scope of Purposes, Goals, and Objectives

Figure 1:1 illustrates the scope of purposes, goals, and objectives. Note that anytime a choice is made options at the next level are diminished or limited. Therefore the parameters of goals are narrower than those of purposes and the parameters of objectives are narrowed by the choice of goals.

Focus on Goals

Goals as statements of generalized intent are designed to meet the expectations of those who directly receive the services provided by the schools and those who work in the schools. There is seldom much disagreement on goals by virtue of their very general nature, but they must meet the expectations of those within the school or college organization as to pertinence and reasonableness. They must appear to be pertinent to the overall purposes of the organization as well as to the specific objectives being carried out by those in the organization, and they must be considered reasonable—goals will not be supported if they do violence to accepted mores of those within or without the organization.

When goals are both pertinent and reasonable, they serve to guide those within the organization as they dispense rewards and sanctions.

Goals can discourage deviate behavior or be used as the basis for rewarding appropriate behavior.

Most organizations, of course, have multiple goals, which usually appear to be congruent as long as one talks about them in general terms. For example, a college might have tthe following goals:

(1) To provide students with a liberal education;
(2) To help students develop an awareness of their environment;
(3) To help students develop as individuals;
(4) To help students understand the contributions of knowledge of the past to solving problems of the present.

All of these appear worthwhile and congruent. However, when they are operationalized it may quickly become apparent that they are not congruent. For example, to help the student develop as an individual may not always be compatible with having him take specific courses designed to help him understand the past and its possible applications to the future. The goal of general education may not always be compatible with what is best for the individual's development at any given time.

Focus on Objectives

Objectives are designed to be quantifiable and must be stated in terms that make them measurable at some point in time. Usually the time span used is relatively short, such as six weeks grading periods or semester grading periods. In schools, such objectives are often stated in behavioral terms, i.e., behavior to be manifested by the students within a space of time. An example: "By the end of six weeks the student will be able to identify and define twenty concepts in sociology, as assigned by by the instructor." Or: "The student will be able to work at least twenty math problems with a minimum success of 80 percent, the problems to include multiplication and addition of fractions." Colleges often state the objectives students should achieve in such terms as: "The student will complete 120 hours with a minimum grade point average of C." It is hoped that these objectives complement the goals of the school or college, but rarely do personnel compare the objectives being carried out with the goals they are supposedly designed to support.

Objectives, because they are concrete, observable, and readily measurable, often become the major focus of teachers in schools and colleges. They lend themselves to demonstration to those outside the institution that it is doing something and is able to measure how well it is doing it. Unfortunately, this tendency to focus on objectives has often led to overemphasis being placed on such things as behavioral objectives, accountability, and standardized testing.

Focus on Congruence of Goals and Objectives

We propose that education decision-makers give much more thought to increasing the congruence between goals and objectives, and that this is likely to be brought about if increasing attention is given to goals. This is not to say that little attention should be given to objectives, but that where major attention now seems to be given to objectives, major attention should instead be paid to goals.

The following example illustrates how a social studies teacher came to focus more on goals than on objectives. His primary goal initially was to help students understand how people of various races and ethnic and religious backgrounds interact with each other, the problems that might interfere with positive interaction, and finally, how these problems could be overcome. At first, he required students to read essays on problems of interaction among groups and then tested them by essay and objective tests to determine the extent to which they had grasped the concepts and facts from their reading. Early in the semester he realized that there was apparently little or no change in the behavior of the students as they interacted with those different from them, although their test scores were adequate and in some cases higher than he had expected. He reviewed the goal he had set for the course and decided that his current objectives might not be contributing substantively to that goal. He devised some role-playing activities and simulation experiences, and used these activities as his primary means of instruction for approximately four weeks. At the end of that period he found distinct changes in the students' behavior and attitudes. He had discovered that although his original objectives *did* contribute to training his students to act and behave like students, they had not significantly contributed to his major goal: to help students understand each other better and therefore interact with each other more effectively.

Single and Multiple Goals and Objectives

In our discussion thus far we have talked about organizations that have multiple goals and objectives. Although most formal organizations are of this kind, some formal organizations have a single objective. After this objective has been met, there is no reason to continue in existence. For example, a superintendent may appoint a school-systemwide curriculum to prepare a report for the visiting evaluation team that will then give its blessing to the operations of the school system. After the curriculum committee has met its objective—the preparation of the report—it disbands.

There are many advantages to the single goal ad hoc kind of committee or formal organization. A single objective organization rarely forms the traditional lines of authority that exist in organizations of a more permanent nature. There is a free flow of both ideas and people, for each newly formed organization has its own group dynamics because of the uniqueness of its task and personnel. The brief life span of such committees or organizations and their task orientation tend to keep organization members more alert, for in more traditional ongoing organizations some members simply bide their time and let others work for them.

Another advantage of the single goal organization is that it does not need to try to resolve possible conflict among goals. For example, a high school may have the following goals:

(1) Students should work to the best of their ability and be evaluated on the basis of their progress rather than on the end product.

(2) Students should score high on standardized tests so they have better opportunities for higher education and the school will have a reputation for excellence.

(3) Students should participate in sports that they enjoy and can participate in throughout their lives.

(4) A winning football team will give unity to the student body and involve parents in the school so that there will be more community support, reflected in the passing of bond issues.

Although all of the goals may be perfectly legitimate, they are not necessarily consistent with each other. In goals (1) and (2), for example, students are not expected to be evaluated only on the basis of results, and yet scores on standardized tests are of great importance. Goals (3) and (4) are also contradictory, for football is not a sport that one can participate in throughout his life. The single goal organization simply avoids such conflict by not having multiple goals.

Behavioral Objectives

This brings us to behavioral objectives—objectives that can be assessed operationally, for to say that objectives should be stated behaviorally is to say that any formal organization and its members are interested in having others *behave* congruently with the formal organization's goals. This means that objectives must be stated with a high degree of concreteness.

The objectives we are most interested in are operational ones, which simply means that they are best indicated in the behavior or actions of members of the formal organization. Objectives in oral or written form may not always be consistent with operational goals. Written goals, for example, are often stated for such reasons as effecting cohesion among members of the formal organization or convincing others outside the organization of their need to support what the organization is doing. In short, they are often used for public relations purposes. Yet such goals are worthy of our attention if one is acquainted with the context in which they are used.[4] Most written goals are stated so generally that everyone in the organization can claim that they are being met, e.g., "Children should be understood as whole persons and their growth should be nurtured."[5]

Goals provide orientation for the future and help the formal organization establish legitimacy for itself. Goals also provide guidelines for assessment of the formal organization's activities.[6] It is a truism that some goals lend themselves more to assessment in behavioral terms than do others. For example, if an objective of the organization is to increase production by 10 percent, one can simply assess what was produced and compare it to new production figures. If a goal of the organization is to have its members relax more through out-of-work activities, progress toward the goal is obviously more difficult to assess. The same kind of problem exists in education, for out-of-school activities, as one example, are more difficult to evaluate.

Nonbehavioral Goals	*Behavioral Goals*
Students should appreciate their environment.	Students should demonstrate through their behavior that: (1) they do not mark or deface the school building; (2) windows are not broken except through normal breakage, such as playing baseball or other similar accidents; (3) they keep the area around the school clean by picking up paper and other similar items.
Students should understand their rights and duties as citizens of the school.	Students should demonstrate through their actions that they are actively engaged in a student government of their own choice: (1) they go through the process of forming their own constitution; (2) they vote for members of the student body for officers in the student organization.

In summary, objectives must be quantifiable and are more likely to be so if they are stated in behavioral terms. In making our appraisal we can look at the actions of those who are expected to meet the objectives, and they in turn can use expected competencies as bench marks in order to gauge their progress. Goals are most effective for public relations purposes and as general guidelines against which to measure objectives.

In recent years, no subject in education has received the attention that behavioral objectives have received. Administrators have returned to their school systems from national and regional meetings armed with the truth: for schools to be accountable to the public—a public that has turned down bond issue after bond issue—curriculum guides must be rewritten so that objectives will be stated in behavioral terms. This emphasis is consistent with a technologically advanced society, for it places a high value on increased productivity —the more the better—and efficiency. Formal education in the United States is seen as an investment that will pay off for the remainder of the student's life. The more technologically perfect the school system, the greater the chance that the investment will pay higher dividends to its clients. Schooling can therefore be seen as a business transaction between clients (taxpayers and students) and educators. When understood in this way, it is desirable if minimum input produces maximum output. As with all behavioral objectives, major emphasis is on the result, or output. The proof is indeed in the pudding rather than in the recipe. This pragmatic view ("If it works, it's good") is clearly consistent with the American experience, for theory has been less important than practice.

Those who support behavioral objectives in our schools and those who criticize such objectives both admit that it is possible, and usually desirable, to state objectives in behavioral terms. This is simply the technical dimension of the issue. Controversy centers rather on whether it is desirable to do so. The argument is largely philosophical. There is a conflict in basic values, belief systems, and philosophic commitments.

The main argument advanced by the critics of behavioral objectives is that the persons expected to reach such objectives have their freedom curtailed, since most, if not all, expected behaviors are predetermined. That is, there is greater emphasis on predetermined and particular results than on the learning process by which many alternatives are generated and experimented with by the learner. It is argued that behavioral objectives produce both a static curriculum and static instruction. Not only is the fun taken out of learning, but the learner is placed in the role of reactor rather than actor—a role clearly inconsistent with democratic rhetoric. This reflects the philosophic position that education is as much an art as a science.

Closely related to this criticism is the view that those who want to state all objectives in behavioral terms emphasize output to the exclusion or near exclusion of input. The learning process is largely affected by intention, and to neglect intention in the interest of result or output is a serious error. Ideally, the critics argue, the teacher, administrator, and others would work with people in the sociopolitical system in order to generate alternatives toward which all could relate (experiment). The results of such experimentation would be very individual or personal and many of the interrelationships could never be analyzed in behavioral terms. The task would be too great and dysfunctional as well, that is, it would miss the point, which is that interaction is often more important than the particular behavioral results of such interaction.

Critics of the behavioral objectives approach also argue that individual differences are subjugated to group norms. The idiosyncratic nature of learning is overlooked in the interest of having all students or others behave in the same way.[7] The bureaucratization of life in the United States is a threat to the uniqueness of persons, and behavioral objectives tend to support sameness rather than uniqueness. Difficulties in individualizing objectives while at the same time stating them behaviorally are reflected in the estimate that a single course could have as many as two thousand objectives, so that the number of individual objectives could amount to as many as sixty thousand if there are thirty students in a class.[8] For this reason many behavioral objectivists look to the computer as the answer, but teachers and others would still have to tailor-make their objectives in order to account for individual and group differences.

It is also argued that the behavioral objectivist acts on the incorrect assumption that learning, knowing, and behaving are the same process.[9] The fact that someone has learned something or knows something does not mean that he will behave in a particular way. The student, for example, may demonstrate that he has learned the concept of multiple causation in a number of ways, many of which the planner may not have taken into account in establishing his behavioral objectives. The teacher may not even be aware of some of the ways the student demonstrates his learning of the concept—especially if the student demonstrates such learning outside of the classroom.

How then can the decision-maker resolve the controversy concerning behavioral objectives? First of all, let us note those instances where both sides agree. It is clear that general, abstract educational goals in curriculum guides and other similar materials are often ignored by educators. School administrators have been the main recipients of any benefits that have accrued from such general objectives, for public relations are often built on general statements that massage the egos of any and all who are recipients of such declarations. "Our school system, administrators, teachers, parents, and others in the community are interested in the whole child, and we do our best daily to do the right thing for boys and girls" is the kind of declaration of intent (goal) that is often useful for public relations purposes and for general guides to behavior within the school, college, or university.

Secondly, all who are interested in educational goals would admit that people within the school as a sociopolitical system have always and will always make judgments about others on the basis of their behavior as it seemingly conforms to the goals of the school. The way a child dresses, the kind of language he uses, the ways in which he cooperates or fails to cooperate, and the degree to which he is actively involved in different activities serve as examples of behavioral cues toward which educators and others react. We can argue as to the superficiality and desirability of taking into account such factors; we cannot argue that they are neglected as behavioral indicators in our schools.

Thirdly, it is both unreasonable and unrealistic to coerce members of a sociopolitical system like a school to state both goals and objectives in the same manner. It is reasonable and realistic to ask members of the school to spell out their philosophic or belief system as it relates to what they are doing and want to do with respect to educational goals. As professionals we should be able to give reasons for our actions and intentions. Fads will come and go, but to be able to go through the process of building a case for what one does or intends to do will always be useful.

Finally, as members of the school as a sociopolitical system we must not only come to terms with our own belief systems with respect to educational ends, but we must also be able to recognize that others in the system often operate with different goal priorities. We must recognize such differences and also be able to deal with them in a personal and political way. If, for example, an administrator returns from a convention and asks us to revise curriculum guides in such a way that all goals are stated behaviorally, we must be able to identify the assumptions on which he is operating and be able to deal with such assumptions and directives in the political arena. In short, we must recognize that he does not differentiate between goals and objectives.

Cognitive and Affective Goals and Objectives

Another thing to note about goals and objectives is that they fall primarily into two instructional domains, commonly identified as cognitive and affective.[10] The cognitive domain emphasizes activities such as remembering and recalling knowledge, thinking, problem solving, and other intellectual processes. The affective domain emphasizes feelings and emotions. The distinction between cognitive and affective is germane to our discussion of formal organizations' goals and objectives, as illustrated in the following list of cognitive and affective goals and objectives.

Cognitive Domain	*Affective Domain*
Parents on a school curriculum committee should identify the most important problems students face in the middle school and propose several alternative solutions to each problem.	Parents should indicate their interest in the curriculum committee findings by attending a meeting where the committee's report will be discussed.
The student should be able to describe what water pollution is, identify some of its causes, and relate water pollution effects on resident animals and/or plants.	The student should demonstrate his *interest* in the water pollution problem by composing music or using some other art form that relates a message on the water pollution theme.

We can see from this list that some desired behaviors emphasize a feeling tone or emotions (affective domain) and others emphasize intellectual tasks (cognitive). Because organizations have as their main goal the manipulation of variables in a situation, they must consider both the affective and cognitive dimensions of human behavior. Television advertising, for example, primarily appeals to one's emotions to manipulate behavior: "Is it possible that even you need mouthwash or a deodorant? Use such-and-such a product!" The element of doubt has been introduced along with a simple remedy prescribed for its resolution. Similar techniques, with varying degrees of boldness, are used by any organization, including the schools. "Do you know how much the average high school graduate makes in a lifetime compared to the dropout?" is an example of the same manipulative technique, only in this case the technique is used by the government and public educators rather than commercial advertisers.

Norms

A second element of sociopolitical systems is norms. Norms, which we might think of as "rules of the game," refer to what is considered acceptable or unacceptable in the system. The following is a list of some of the norms that the formal organization of one school, here called School 101, supports:

(1) Students should attend school for nine months of the year, except during holidays or when they have a legitimate excuse, such as an illness.

(2) Smoking is not allowed on school grounds but students who smoke behind the gym and adults who smoke at school board meetings will not be asked to stop doing so.

(3) General guidelines for a dress code say that a student should be neat and clean but the only time that a student is sent home for dress code violations is when he or she is barefoot.

(4) The student body gives a great deal of support to the football team as evidenced by pep rallies and cheering at games, but gives very little support to the swimming team as evidenced by few spectators at swimming meets.

(5) No formal dances are held at the school but students occasionally dance after extracurricular events, such as a hayride or football game.

It is clear from the list that some norms are *stated* and others are *tacit*. "Smoking is not allowed on school grounds" is stated in the school handbook, but in reality students can smoke behind the gym at any time and adults may smoke in the school board's meeting room. These exceptions to the stated rule are simply understood and are therefore the basis for the actions of members of the sociopolitical system. They are tacitly acceptable.

Norm conflict exists when the "rules of the game" as operationally defined by the formal organization in its actions are not acceptable to informal organizations in the sociopolitical system. For example, in School 101 teachers and administrators tried for four months to police the school grounds for smoking violators but found their surveillance ineffective due to an ingenious lookout system devised by the students. The formal organization therefore decided to look the other way and simply ignore infractions of the rule. Their norms were once again consistent with the norms of the informal organization of students who were smoking behind the gym. The same kind of situation existed with respect to the school's dress code. The original code said that skirts should not be more than three inches above the knee and shirts had to have pockets (an effort to eliminate T-shirts on school grounds). This code was resisted by almost all the student body, which reacted to a few students being sent home for dress violations. The next day there were mass violations of the dress code. The administration could not send home the entire student body, and negotiations between the student government and the administration resulted in the new general statement, "A student should be neat and clean," but it was also agreed between students and administration that students who came to school barefoot would be sent home.

It has also been reported that schools that have established student courts to have peer disapproval weigh on offenders have disbanded such courts when judges and juries let off offenders who pleaded temporary insanity. In this case an arm of the formal organization, the student court, followed the letter of the law too closely.

We can see from these examples that norms are not always precise as to what is acceptable, but instead often set the parameters of acceptable behavior. Those who support the norms of a system try to maintain the boundaries so that the system will not be threatened. We have noted that people operate at different levels of consciousness as to their goals. This is also true with respect to norms. Members of a sociopolitical organization may behave as if they are well aware that they have conformed to the standards or norms of the formal organization. Yet if they are interviewed they may not appear to have a high level of consciousness in their observance of such standards. Interviewing members of a sociopolitical system is one way to gauge the level of consciousness members have about their conformity to the formal organization's norms. Another way is to use simple observation to see if people behave as though they are conscious of their relationship to the formal organization's standards. A third way is to look at stated norms, both written and verbalized.

Rewards and Sanctions

Norms and the parameters of acceptable behavior are enforced by rewards and sanctions. The term *sanctions* is used here synonymously with punishments, that is, they are negative sanctions. The formal organization positively reinforces behavior that it deems acceptable and sanctions unacceptable behavior. As it is impossible for the formal organization always to predict how people will react to stimuli designed to reward or sanction, the organization must instead rely on what it thinks will probably happen when particular rewards are given and sanctions are invoked. The kinds of rewards or sanctions, the way they are presented, and the timing of the introduction of the stimulus determine whether or not the formal organization has been successful in using a reward or sanction. Obviously, future actions of those who have been rewarded or sanctioned will indicate the degree of success the formal organization has achieved.

Rewards and sanctions are sometimes planned and at other times are spontaneous. This again relates to the level of consciousness of those who direct such rewards and sanctions. If a reward or sanction is spontaneous it is usually a good indication that a norm is internalized, held to be dear, by those who directed the reward or sanction.

Rewards and sanctions have varying degrees of subtlety. They may be as direct as "You surely are a good teacher," or as subtle as a passing smile. Both verbal and nonverbal cues indicate positive and negative feelings members of a formal organization have toward each other and others in the sociopolitical system.

The following list indicates some of the rewards and sanctions School 101's administration employed.

Rewards

During the school year's opening meeting the superintendent conveyed his support of the teaching staff by:

(1) Reminding them of the large across-the-board increase in salaries he had secured for them in the previous spring;

(2) Saying they were selected from a large number of applicants, thereby indicating the faith the system had in them; and

(3) Promising to try to secure increased hospital benefits for teachers and their families during the school year.

(His nonverbal cues during his talk were received well by the teachers. He smiled, was pleasant, and conveyed his faith in the staff.)

In a specially called meeting the principal congratulated the teachers for the excellent report written by the regional accreditation team. He summarized some of the main points in the report and indicated with both verbal and nonverbal actions his approval of the teaching staff.

Sanctions

The principal in an effort to get teachers to work on time stood by the front door of the school to "greet" teachers who came late.

The superintendent verbally criticized teachers at a faculty meeting for failing to give adequate support to a school bond proposal.

The assistant principal, with the aid of the principal's secretary, sent a memorandum to teachers castigating those who failed to hand in the first hour attendance reports.

The principal sent a memorandum to teachers asking them to stop using the mimeograph machine, since they were wasting paper. They were asked to give their work to secretaries who would do the mimeographing for them.

Power

Rewards and *sanctions* are used to enforce *norm* compliance so that *objectives* of the formal organization can be met. Central to all of these elements of sociopolitical systems is the element of *power*. Power may be defined as control over others. It reflects the degree to which an individual or group affects the actions of others. For purposes of our discussion we have identified two kinds of power: *authority* and *influence*. Authority is the legitimate right as determined by the formal organization to control the actions of others, while influence is of a less legal or formal nature. Influence is usually also less overt and depends instead on the persuasive abilities of an individual or group. We can therefore say that authority is based on one's legalized role in the formal organization, whereas influence is earned through interpersonal relations. Authority does not exist in an informal organization like the second hour coffee group but is very important in the formal organization, as evidenced by the superintendent having more authority than the principal and the principal having more authority than the vice-principal, and so forth.

Because of its personal nature, influence is more difficult to trace. Given the personalities of the vice-principal and the principal, it is possible, although not probable, that the vice-principal has more influence on the superintendent than does the principal. The idiosyncratic nature of influence patterns is evident in the example of a teacher who is a fishing and hunting friend of the superintendent. He has easy communicational access to the superintendent because of this special relationship and can influence the superintendent more by giving him five minutes of information than can the principal, whose office is directly across the hall from the superintendent's office.

Information input is a key to understanding influence patterns, for all information is selective and biased to the value system of the informer. In School 101, a new principal assumed his duties and his orientation to the new position was provided mainly by the two counselors, whose offices were next to the principal's office, and by the principal's secretary. Immediate proximity to the principal gave the secretary and counselors untold advantages in influencing decisions made by the principal. A tacit agreement was worked out between the principal and his secretary for screening candidates for teaching positions. At first the principal took information provided by the secretary as to manners, personal appearance, and general bearing of candidates who asked for application forms. With time, the principal let the secretary do the screening of the candidates she felt wouldn't fit into the school. Those candidates who didn't show the proper respect and/or appeared slovenly because of their dress or long hair never got past the secretary. Their applications were simply "lost," with the principal's unspoken approval, and they were not interviewed for positions in the school.

Prospective and inservice teachers can profit from studying the authority and influence patterns that exist in different school systems. The following sources will help the reader in his inquiry:

School

Classrooms
Library
Audiovisual room
Counseling and nurse facilities
Cafeteria
Faculty lounge
Teaching staff (degree, stability, dress, etc.)
Psychologist, speech therapist, and others
Administrative and office staff and offices
Office secretaries, counseling secretaries, and custodians
Parents
Curriculum (overt and hidden)
Extra curricular activities (band, vocal, athletics, dramatics, clubs)
Faculty and student handbooks
School newspapers
Yearbook
P.T.A.
Discipline methods (punitive, corrective consistent with learning theory)
Organizations (A.F.T., N.E.A., and others)
Physical appearance of school
Transportation methods
Summer programs

District

District paper
District office
School board
Superintendent
Financial status of district (salary schedule, fringe benefits)
Information and application forms sent to applicants

Community

Local newspapers
Personal contacts
Areas outside the school where students spend their time

Residential areas

Business areas and types of businesses
Growth of area
Educational facilities in the community (universities, colleges, etc.)

Chance

Formal organizations emphasize rational process. Every effort is made to see that activities of people are coordinated so that the events that occur in the organization should be predictable—little is left to chance. In practice, however, chance plays a major role in what actually takes place. By chance we mean events which the organization's rational processes are not designed to accommodate. Chance is an unanticipated occurence that may be either good or bad as far as the people in the organization are concerned.

Chance serves as the basis for an organizational paradox. The more rationally and systematically organizations are structured, the less they are likely to be able to meet changing conditions. The more conditions change, the more likely it is that chance will occur. Thus, all formal organizations must and do emphasize rationality as the basis for a systematic approach to the solution of problems, but the more systematic and rational they become, the less likely they are able to deal effectively with chance occurrences.

An example of chance and the inability of highly rational and prescriptive procedures to deal with it can be seen from the events that took place at a university a few years back. It was spring; many students were on campus, not yet having left for the spring break. A rock group had set up amplifiers and was entertaining some six hundred students gathered on the lawn in front of the student union, when word spread that a dormitory had been raided by police looking for drugs. Many of the students began walking toward the dorm. None seemed in a particularly hostile mood, though some made statements about what they would do to the "pigs." As they moved toward the dorm, two campus policemen blocked their way and read to them the regulation passed by the board of trustees concerning student gatherings. There was an exchange of words between the police and some of the student leaders, for by now the group had leaders—or at least spokesmen. The campus police then retired from the scene, and following their formal rules and procedures called in the local police. Within thirty minutes there was a confrontation between the local police and the students. Several students were arrested, and several injured.

In the investigation that followed, it was determined that the likelihood of the students doing anyone harm was remote and that the campus police, though acting strictly according to the rules, had probably precipitated the incident. Soon thereafter the rules for handling student gatherings were changed, and most prescription was taken out of them. The new rules stated that only in the event human life was imminently threatened was any force to be applied, and that such a decision could be made only by the president of the university, or, in his absence, the vice-president.

Some on campus were uncomfortable with the new rule because they felt it did not give sufficient guidance, but the university administration believed it better to opt for flexibility and whatever ambiguity might result than for prescriptive rules and regulations.

Chance, then, can play a major role in organizational decision-making, but the organization that attempts to prescribe how one should react to chance events does something that has not been done wisely and cannot be. Those who would deal with chance effectively must have a high tolerance for ambiguity and be comfortable in the face of the unknown.

In chapters 2, 3, and 4 the reader will see examples of organizations that have placed much stress on rationality to make their environments more predictable. To the extent that chance occurs, prescription is likely to fail. It is indeed paradoxical that the very rules and regulations that are designed to help people deal rationally with events can in the face of chance become dysfunctional, and in fact cause people to handle events irrationally.

Informal Organizations

The main emphasis in this chapter has been on formal organizations and how they try to influence members within the sociopolitical system. The actions of formal organizations are more predictable than are those of informal organizations. Formal organizations are forced to plan to achieve as high a degree of efficiency as possible. This means that it is much easier to study the elements of formal organizations and their relationships with each other. (Objectives of informal organizations, for example, are less clear-cut, and access to resources of the formal organization is at best difficult, at worst impossible.)

Informal organizations are not as predictable as formal organizations, and formal rules and regulations are of little interest to the members. In fact, members of informal organizations learn rather quickly how to slide around formal rules and regulations, which goes to demonstrate that they spend a good deal of their time reacting to the elements of formal organizations. Because members of informal organizations do not have authority by virtue of this membership, they must instead rely on *influence* as a source of power. As soon as the informal organization engages in systematic planning, it in essence becomes a formal organization with its own elements.

The impact of informal organizations on members of the sociopolitical system is usually incidental if not accidental. This impact depends on the formal organization's recognition of the activities of the informal organization, and such recognition is at some times difficult and at other times impossible to get. (It should be noted that informal organizations tap members of the formal organization for their membership. Therefore an educator is a member of the larger formal organization and smaller informal groups at the same time.)

Although it is more difficult to speak of elements of informal organizations than elements of formal organizations, the following case study of an informal organization, the second hour coffee group in School 101, will demonstrate that such elements do exist in informal organizations.

The main goal of the second hour coffee group was to relax away from their students. As a result of this goal there was informal agreement that controversial subjects would not be discussed. It was also agreed that members would not simply sit around and gripe about the administration. Both of these tacitly accepted agreements were *norms* of the group. On one occasion a new teacher threatened these norms; she started complaining about the administration's incompetence. The other five people in the group *sanctioned* her by isolating her from the group. They did not initiate conversation with her and didn't seem to pay much attention to anything she had to say. When she got the message and stopped complaining, they were much nicer to her and again included her in the group, thereby *rewarding* her.

All groups need some resources and are displeased when they are short of *resources.* This situation occurred in the second hour coffee group when they ran out of coffee. Outside of this one incident, they were content with their meeting place and with their informally accepted norms.

Conclusion

In this chapter we have identified elements common to all formal organizations in sociopolitical systems, with special emphasis on educational organizations as sociopolitical systems. We hope that the reader has acquired the analytic tools necessary to understand and work more effectively. In the following chapters we will use the concepts discussed in the present chapter to see how members of the organizations coordinate elements of sociopolitical systems to achieve their objectives.

A Self-Inventory of Beliefs on Functions of Educational Organizations

Name______________________________ Section__________Date________

We would like you to participate in the following exercise in order for you to see where you stand before reading chapter 2. After you have read chapter 2 and discussed ideas from it, you may wish to go through the exercise once again to see if any changes have occurred in your thinking.

To record your responses to the following statements, write the code on the right side of the page. If you strongly agree with a statement, write SA next to it; if you agree, write A; if you disagree, write D; and if you strongly disagree, write SD.

(1) The teacher is an independent person who can for the most part do what he or she pleases once the classroom door is closed. ______

(2) Educational organizations are fortunate compared to many other organizations, for they are subject to little influence from government(s). ______

(3) Since educational organizations and educators are largely independent, the major obstacle to making changes in them is teachers' perceptions, which are conservative about change. ______

(4) Educational administrators are usually bureaucrats, for they cater to governmental officials, such as members of the governing board, immediately above them on the bureaucratic ladder. ______

(5) Unlike administrators, teachers are professionals who deal with public reaction after they make their decisions rather than anticipating public reaction. ______

(6) Administrators have more in common with politicians in their occupational role than do teachers. ______

(7) Fortunately for local school board districts, the state government has a good deal of influence on them but federal laws have little or no effect on them. ______

(8) The greater the influence of government on an organization, the more bureaucratic the organization will be. ______

(9) It is of little value for the decision-maker in schools to make a distinction between governance functions and curriculum and instruction. ______

(10) Schools, like hospitals, have bureaucratic and professional structures operating side by side, with the professional structure clearly having the prime authority. ______

(11) Students should be involved in the setting of objec-

tives and goals, but not in establishing the means for reaching them. ______

(12) All organizations confine their members, which means that they force them to be in certain places for a specified period of time regardless of their personal wishes. ______

(13) Teachers, unlike other professionals, tailor their confinement practices to the individual needs and desires of their clients. ______

(14) Administrators usually interpret board decisions more liberally than the board would and teachers interpret administrator decisions more liberally than do administrators. ______

(15) Teachers usually define training skills such as reading, writing, speaking, and modes of thinking in much the same way as their students do, adjusting such skills to the socioeconomic and family backgrounds of students. ______

(16) Curriculum materials, like textbooks, rarely reflect the real interests of students. ______

(17) Minority group students, that is, those students who do not have the background or interest to become successful students, should nevertheless be forced to learn skills in order to "get ahead" when they graduate. ______

(18) Indoctrination (influencing a person so that he behaves as you want him to behave without questioning whether or not that is the way he wants to or should behave) is employed in highly structured organizations such as the armed forces but is rarely used in educational organizations. ______

(19) Students have a good deal to say about the way they are sorted or classified in educational organizations, since the "cream" in any organization tends to rise to the top. ______

(20) The confinement, indoctrination, sorting, and training functions as practiced by educational organizations are consistent with the objective of providing the conditions for personal or self-development as defined by most students. ______

Notes for Chapter 1

1. See, for example, Amitai Etzioni, *Modern Organizations* (Englewood Cliffs, N.J.: Prentice-Hall, 1964), pp. 20-31.

2. This is the paradox of any revolutionary organization. When it achieves the power it feels it needs, it becomes the new establishment. Anticapitalists who become rich from writing revolutionary books are a case in point.

3. See A. H. Maslow, *Motivation and Personality* (New York: Harper and Brothers, 1954), chapters 4, 5, and 8.

4. To know, for example, that goals stated in a newsletter to parents are not to be taken at face value, but instead are designed for public relations purposes, is useful information, for it tells us that good public relations is valued as a goal by those within the formal organization.

5. For criticism of goals stated in nonbehavioral terms, see Robert F. Mager, *Preparing Instructional Objectives* (Belmont, Calif.: Fearon Press, 1962).

6. Etzioni, *Modern Organizations*, p. 5.

7. George F. Kneller, "Behavioral Objectives? No!" *Educational Leadership* 29, no. 5 (February 1972): 398.

8. Ibid.

9. Ibid.

10. Benjamin Bloom et al., *Taxonomy of Educational Objectives*, vol. 1, *Cognitive Domain* (New York: David McKay Co., 1956), and vol. 2, *Affective Domain* (New York: David McKay Co., 1964). (Bloom and his colleagues also identified a third domain, the psychomotor domain, but it is incidental to the present discussion.)

(2)

Functions of Educational Organizations

Educational organizations perform discrete functions for their clients. In this chapter we describe the functions that educational organizations perform, not necessarily those functions they claim to perform. We have identified these functions as confinement, training, indoctrination, sorting, and providing the conditions for personal or self-development. Here we focus the reader's attention on how such functions are performed in various settings, and the degree of emphasis given to each function.

Although confinement no longer is carried out in colleges or universities except in a few antiquated places of total female enrollment, the colleges do perform a function that is similar to confinement, which we would characterize as incubation. Our society, possibly more than any other, encourages and provides for a youth culture. Colleges offer to approximately 50 percent of all high school graduates an incubative environment in which students are encouraged to focus on the world of the university as the real world, and attempts are made to prevent the world outside from impinging on the activities of the students. Of course, in recent years students have indicated little satisfaction with this function, but most colleges still act as if incubation were a critical function for them to perform.

Colleges do perform the other four functions for their students—i.e., training, indoctrination, sorting, and providing the conditions for personal or self-development. We have discussed how elementary and secondary schools perform these functions, and have given a few references to the ways colleges perform them. Chapters 3 and 4 deal with schools and institutions of higher education as bureaucratic organizations. We discuss instruction in those organizations, and not other services they provide, and compare the bureaucratic model of organization to the professional model of organization. Although the bureaucratic model may be appropriate for many governance functions of schools and colleges, it is for the most part inappropriate for providing effective instruction if we accept that instruction does for students what schools and colleges claim it does. We propose a new model for educational organizations, a model that draws heavily on the professional model for instruction while retaining the bureaucratic model for governance.

Confinement

Confinement simply means that a person must be in a certain place for a specified period of time regardless of his personal wishes about being there. Schools confine students in a number of ways, some prescribed by law (that is, the state legislature, the state board of education, and the local school board), some by school rules and regulations, and others by the teacher in the classroom.

State law requires students between certain ages from five or six to sixteen or eighteen to attend school for a given number of days, usually 180.[1] One may be surprised at the minimal prescription for confinement by state government by comparison with all the restrictions placed on students in schools. Obviously, then, the source of these restrictions rests primarily with the local school board, local school administrators, and teachers. Teachers and school administrators often deny the responsibility for many confinement practices and point to the state as the "villain." School boards effect rules and regulations that in fact have the full force of law because the school board is legally the official agent of the state. For example, in response to citizen complaints about students crowding business establishments during the lunch hour, a local school board passed a measure requiring students to remain in school during the lunch hour. This rule had the full force of state law, subject only to legislative or judicial action. (This regulation would probably not have been passed had the school officials offered the board a solution other than the general prescription confining all students in the school.)

The school board in any school system plays an important role in refining laws passed in the state legislature by establishing rules and regulations designed to meet local conditions. This local school board in interpreting local conditions required that no student could leave the school grounds during school hours except *under the supervision of a school official.* The school administration interpreted this to mean that no student could leave the premises during the school day *unless accompanied by a teacher.* The teachers interpreted this to mean that no student could leave the school during school hours *unless all students in the class left for a school-sponsored activity,* for a teacher cannot teach classes and accompany students away from the school at the same time. The organizational principle that explains what happened is simply that as the initial rule or regulation filters down a bureaucratic hierarchy, it becomes increasingly prescriptive and hence restrictive. What began as a governance principle eventually came to dictate what could and could not happen in curriculum and instruction. The teacher could not individualize instruction to the extent that a student could go to museums, libraries, or other appropriate places, for to do so would in the teacher's judgment violate the rule.

We will now apply the professional rather than bureaucratic organizational model to the 180-day state government requirement. The law passed by the legislature is not particularly restrictive and can be accepted as given. The initial professional judgment entered when the school board made its decision. The school board had experienced negative public reaction to the behavior of some students who left the school grounds during school hours and frequented places which in the judgment of some citizens should not be frequented. As a local governmental body the school board had to respond to public reaction. If its response reflected the professional judgments of school personnel, it would not have prescribed a restriction on the behavior on all students, but would instead have left to the judgment of school personnel the appropriate courses of action for the individual students involved. The appropriate school board action would have been to ask school administrators and teachers to see that students who left school during school hours had specific and well-planned activities consistent with the aims of curriculum and instruction.

The main barrier to such professionalism, in our judgment, rests with teachers and administrators whose past experience and present comfort leads them to perceive the educative process as being most effectively carried out in a programmatic and prescribed fashion consistent with the bureaucratic model of organization. Since the prime concern of schools is the production of successful students or incipient scholars, and since successful students are judged by their performance in traditional school activities, the more students are confined in schools the more likely they are to be judged as successful.

We can see from the previous discussion that there is a pronounced tendency to deal with a problem of misbehavior by a few by restricting the behavior of all. This can become almost pathological, so that if the chewing of gum by one student is so "gross" that it annoys other students or the teacher, the teacher may well rule that no students may chew gum.[2]

The reader should not be misled by our criticism of many confinement activities to think that we are rejecting confinement categorically. Obviously there are times when students need to meet schedules and be supervised; this is especially the case the younger the child is (as one teacher facetiously remarked, "How can I teach him to read if I can't catch him?"). The proper role of confinement is determined by the specific purpose(s) at hand and depends on such factors as student needs and instructional goals. Such judgments are best made by teachers as professionals and should not be bureaucratically prescribed for all.

Confinement has a role to play in both the governance of schools and in curriculum and instruction, but it is the means to more important ends rather than an end in itself. Confinement must be consistent with (1) the individual needs of students and (2) the overall ends of curriculum and instruction. Thus one should employ different models of confinement in different situations, so that the choice can always be flexible and subject to revision. A comparative analysis of organizations and how they use confinement may be helpful to the reader; we can use hospitals and prisons as examples. Prisons confine all inmates but some are placed in intensive security, some in regular confinement, some are trustees, some are placed on honor farms, and some are parolees. In confining patients as a means to treat them, hospitals use several models including intensive care, regular care without privileges to leave the room, regular care with an opportunity to walk or move about the floor, and out patient treatment.

Schools, however, tend to use one confinement model for all students at a particular grade level rather than take into account individual needs for and reactions to confinement. For example, couldn't schools use the outpatient model, the trustee model, the intensive care model, and the parolee model, and other models that have flexibility built into them? Some schools presently do use different models for confinement that take into account individual differences and preferences. Some schools, for example, have distributive education whereby students work half a day and go to school half a day, and other, more open, schools use different confinement models.

Training

For schools to produce successful students or incipient scholars, it is necessary to train the students in such a way that they acquire the skills and modes of behavior consistent with the role of successful student. The skills that students are expected to learn can be categorized into four major areas: (1) reading, (2) writing, (3) speaking, and (4) modes of thinking.

Occasionally we hear someone say about a child, "He can't read." What is really meant is that he can't read the materials he is expected to read in a technically precise way. For example, he can't read the textbook so that he is able to answer the teacher's questions in a manner the teacher finds acceptable. The same student reads the sports page daily and knows the batting averages of the top ten hitters in the American and National Leagues, and he can summarize what happened in a particular baseball game described in newspaper articles. Another student described as a nonreader can read automobile repair manuals and repair cars on the basis of information he thus acquired. What is obvious is that the schools define reading very narrowly and accept as evidence of reading ability only those things that promote good grades in schools. Good grades are the hallmark of the successful student or incipient scholar.

As with reading, only certain kinds of writing are encouraged and rewarded, specifically a technical kind of writing designed to respond to teacher-made or adopted (for example, from the textbook) questions, and essays documented in scholarly style. Emphasis is on the mechanics and style of writing rather than on content or what is said. In one secondary school there was in effect the "banned error rule." This meant that any paper written in an English class received an automatic F if it had more than three banned errors, which included, for example, misspelled words and common grammatical errors. Writing in schools is acceptable or proper only if it fits the teacher's idea of what a successful student should write. This norm excludes the view of writing as a skill by which a person can express his ideas to someone he wants to express them to, that is, as communication.

Many good elementary and secondary teachers, unhappy with writing as an imposed chore, encourage their students to communicate what is important to them in a style appropriate to the person the student wishes to direct his ideas toward. A common beginning-of-school practice in many elementary and secondary language arts and English classes is to write an essay on "My Summer Vacation." This practice implies that (1) the student's summer vacation is something he really wants to communicate about, and (2) the student wants to direct such communication to the teacher. An alternative to this practice was initiated by a fourth grade teacher during the first week of school. She asked each student to write on the subject of his choice, and to direct such writing to whomever he chose. The teacher and other students then worked in the roles of consultant and editor, helping the writer to clarify his ideas and communicate these ideas more effectively. There were two basic assumptions behind this teacher's approach. First, all students should know that writing is a valuable means of communication out of school as well as in school, and, secondly, not all students may become proficient in the technical aspects of writing required by most teachers, but all should develop proficiency in expressing ideas to whomever they wish.

The school as a closed sociopolitical system has its own language designed to promote its paramount goal: the production of incipient scholars. (Open and closed systems are discussed at the conclusion of this section.) To some extent this language is appropriate for other social systems in which the student participates. For example, if the student comes from a family all of whom are college educated, the language of the school will probably be quite appropriate for family conversations at the dinner table, less appropriate for his discussions with friends when they discuss dating, and totally inappropriate for his job as a gas station attendant. On the other hand, if his family has not known much success in the schools, or neither parent has finished high school, the preferred school language will probably be totally inappropriate for his conversation at the dinner table.

Acceptable modes of thinking are segmented in our schools, and the higher the grade level the more segmented they become. A second grader knows that pollution comes from smokestacks, cars, and trash, that pollution is bad or undesirable and he and others should do something about it, e.g., not litter. He has unknowingly applied scientific concepts, philosophical or ethical concepts, social concepts, and political concepts. At this stage of his development he has not been forced to compartmentalize his thinking along disciplinary lines. This he will learn to do as he progresses through the school system and becomes a more successful student or incipient scholar. Unfortunately, as he learns to think in disciplinary segments, he is likely to lose sight of the overall problem, pollution, and the relevance of the disciplines to solving the problem.

X In effect, schools teach students to think convergently rather than divergently. That is, students learn to respond systematically to an imposed set of questions rather than look around them, analyze what they see, ask their own questions, and synthesize their findings into their own framework.

The rationale that supports the development of the four training skills has the following common elements or characteristics:

(1) The cognitive aspect of learning is given much greater emphasis than the affective aspect of learning. Intellective tasks such as recalling and remembering bits of information receive greater attention than the emotional or feeling side of learning. From a practical standpoint this means that schools place much emphasis on an impersonal approach to problems and their solutions, and the problems are for the most part outside the experience and interest of the

students. For example, the student may spend much time discussing relations with Red China but little or no time discussing relations with his black neighbor. The macrocosmic problems of the world are treated in a detached and antiseptic way even though they are considered of paramount importance in the curriculum. Essential parts of relations between nations, such as power struggles between leaders and their respective supporters, are often salved over or neglected and in their place bizarre but interesting bits of information are substituted ("Let me tell you about the tea ceremony, class"), simplistic moral judgments, and mini-sermons. The microcosmic problems in the student's immediate world are too often neglected.

(2) In inculcating training skills, schools place emphasis, for the most part, on the written rather than on the spoken word or other forms of communication—especially nonverbal communication. This is done despite the estimate that adults rely on the written word for 10 percent, or less, of their communication in their business and social lives. This demonstrates once again that the school is a closed system, for it doesn't relate to certain elements of systems outside it, such as the student's family, his work organization if he has a part-time job, and his social groups. It does, however, relate to his continued progress in a formal educational system and to his future life's work in the event that he elects a professional career, and particularly if he chooses the profession of teaching.

(3) The school encourages a passive rather than an active involvement by the student. This is demonstrated in terms of the learning styles emphasized as well as in the lack of emphasis on student involvement in applying what he learns to situations outside the school. The passive role that students learn to play is illustrated in the story of the first grader at Cape Canaveral whose class was discussing some basic principle of rocket propulsion. The teacher asked the students to decide how they might learn more on the subject. One youngster suggested that they might visit the space center two miles away, a second child suggested that the class might look at books about rockets, and the class voted overwhelmingly in favor of the books.

Another example of the failure to apply school learning to situations outside school occurred in a seventh grade science class. The biology teacher spent six weeks attempting to teach the concept of classification. The major assignment was to classify twenty different organisms using a fixed biological classification system. One of the students who labored diligently over the assignment, and completed it successfully, told her father when asked that she didn't have the foggiest notion what classification meant. She saw no relationship between the concept and the fact that she had classified phenomena daily on both a single and multivariable basis, classifying objects by size, texture, color, and a host of other variables. If the teacher's objective was really to teach students the concept of classification, it is doubtful that he accomplished his goal. If, on the other hand, the teacher's aim was to require students to commit to memory a fixed and already known biological classification, it was hardly worth the time and effort. Systems are constantly upgraded and/or discontinued. They can also be referred to without committing them to memory.

(4) The school assumes that a student's ideas are good or valid only if they are supported by an authority considered to be legitimate by the school. For example, a ghetto student whose language serves him well in his daily life outside school finds that the same language is unacceptable in the classroom because school authorities say it fails to communicate. His own experience to the contrary, he is taught that there is only one "right" way to communicate.

This kind of experience is repeated time after time when the student's own ideas come into conflict with authorities such as textbooks, workbooks, teacher biases, examinations, and community mores. In examinations, for example, the teacher decides what is important, and whether or not one has successfully demonstrated that he has learned what is considered important.

As a result of previous experience and present interests, many students do not value learning training skills such as reading and writing. They do not value becoming incipient scholars. Schools are presently taught in such a way that they are biased against those who do not have an interest in becoming successful students or incipient scholars as a result of their background and its relationship to what they value. This is why we say that schools are closed, a world to themselves. If all youngsters accepted the incipient scholar model, schools would be eminently successful and the world outside the school would be very different.

What is clear is that our society values the incipient scholar or successful student model for these reasons: (1) it is the model we are most familiar with, and tradition supports it; (2) the model strongly reinforces the socioeconomic status quo in our society, since those who are successful in the larger society are most likely to have continued success for themselves and their children, and the converse is also true—the unsuccessful and their children will continue not to make it in the larger society; and (3) an advanced technological society such as ours requires a highly trained manpower pool, for we must have many doctors, lawyers, engineers, teachers, and others who are technically trained to maintain and increase the benefits of improved technology. Our society has charged the schools with the task of providing this training. Again, the school as a governmental organization reflects public opinion.[3]

Our society expects the schools to train students, but does not fully explain the degree of emphasis given to particular training skills or the manner in which such skills are taught. To more fully understand the status quo we must return to the primary objective schools support. Since the primary objective is the production of successful students or incipient scholars, it follows that students are trained to succeed in schools. Those in authority in schools may well claim that they support other objectives, such as individual self-development, good citizenship, and worthy home membership, but those objectives certainly take second place to producing successful students.

What are the alternatives available to those who are disenchanted with the present approach to training skills? There need to be models other than the incipient scholar model—models with different goal priorities than those presently held. Some of these models are already supported by various curriculum experts and have titles, e.g., human relations, humanistic education, and self-development. These titles indicate the ineffectiveness of the bureaucratic model for curriculum and instruction, since it focuses on a systematic and predetermined program designed to achieve agreed on and quantifiable objectives. The bureaucratic model will not effectively accommodate the alternative of human relations, for example, for the means for reaching the objectives of the human relations model are not predetermined, the objectives themselves are not immediately quantifiable, and causation between means and ends is obviously not known.

Indoctrination

Indoctrination is the third major function that educational organizations perform for their clients. Theodore Brameld, philosopher of education, defines indoctrination in the following way:

> Indoctrination is the method of formal or informal teaching and learning presupposing the possession by the teacher of a body of more or less unified belief which is taught to the learner as so fundamentally true and desirable as to pre-suppose that all alternative doctrines are, by comparison, considered to be fundamentally untrue and undesirable.[4]

In other words, indoctrination means that you influence a person to behave as you want him to behave without even questioning whether or not that is the way *he* wants to or should behave.

There are principles that explain how an individual or a group attempts to indoctrinate others. Rewards are given for appropriate behavior, sanctions are applied for inappropriate behavior, and a general environment is created in which the behavior to be instilled becomes second nature to those being indoctrinated. A good example of this is United States Marine Corps boot camp training, which is structured to indoctrinate recruits to believe that they are no longer individuals in the sense that they were as civilians, for everything they do now reflects not only on them but also on their unit and the entire Marine Corps. This is especially critical for combat duty; studies of combat units have demonstrated that men in battle who think of their individual welfare rather than that of the unit tend to have a higher incidence of "battle fatigue." It is also the case that the efficiency of a combat unit is highly related to the selflessness of the individual, and to his commitment to the welfare of the unit as a whole. This isn't to be reasoned and debated, but is to become second nature to the marine.

During the Korean War, mass punishment was employed to teach the lesson that if one errs, all suffer. For example, if one recruit left his bed unmade, all recruits were required to make beds during their "free" hours. Another punishment required the entire platoon to spend extra hours marching if one or two recruits failed to execute all of the drill maneuvers properly. On the other hand, the entire platoon was rewarded with liberty or leave when it marched well or performed well as a unit. Constant reference was made by officers in lectures and "informal" remarks that no marine was ever deserted by another marine, and if you saw a marine in trouble you didn't ask the reason why but immediately went to his aid. No officer ever officially advised his recuits to discipline a recalcitrant recruit, but there was a tacit understanding that it was to everyone's advantage for a person who was consistently "out of step" to be taken aside and shown the error of his ways—usually by the more physical members of the platoon. These are but a few of the techniques employed by one organization to indoctrinate its members.

Schools have distinct systems of rewards to promote behavior consistent with their norms, and sanctions to discourage behavior that deviates from the norms. The overall activities of the school create an environment that encourages and reinforces desirable behavior while at the same time providing little opportunity for the exhibition of undesirable behavior. One way to create such an environment is by filling the student's schedule with activities designed to promote the school's goals, though not necessarily the student's goals. This gives the student as little time as possible to pursue his or her individual desires. In effect, you keep the student so busy doing what you want him to do that he doesn't have the time or inclination to behave differently. (Or as the Puritans would have it, "Idle hands are the devil's handmaiden.")

The following are some of the rewards given students:

Good grades;

Membership on the honor roll;

Special positions, such as student monitors, offices in student government, and teacher aides;

Exemptions from taking examinations;

Eligibility for special clubs an; organizational activities;

Subtle and not so subtle attitudes expressed by teachers and administrators.

The following are some of the sanctions directed against students:

Poor grades;

Denial of normal school privileges and special privileges;

Punishments, ranging from detention to expulsion;

Subtle and not so subtle behavior by teachers and administrators showing disapproval.

Some things that students are indoctrinated to believe are obvious, such as, do well in your studies and you'll get ahead, formal education is necessary for economic advancement, hard work will result in good grades. In this section we will focus on the less obvious, and certainly questionable and perhaps insidious, beliefs students are expected to accept.

Schools attempt to instill in students an attitude toward authority which will result in unquestioning compliance with rules, regulations, and pronouncements from teachers and administrators. The answer to a question is right or wrong as judged by the teacher's definition of "rightness" and "wrongness." The facts that the student can't leave the room without a pass and that the school restrooms are locked between classes to curtail smokers are not to be questioned, for they are school rules. It is paradoxical that schools claim to prepare students for citizenship in a democracy, which requires a willingness and ability to question those in authority, yet demand for the most part just the opposite. (Recent events in our schools indicate that students are less willing to submit to many indoctrination practices, but most school officials still seem intent on effecting such practices.)

Democratic rhetoric also has it that schools should teach attitudes of cooperation and concern for others. In fact, students are seldom rewarded with the currency of the school for taking this rhetoric seriously. Jimmy Jones and Tommy Smith are close friends and sit next to each other during an arithmetic test. Jimmy knows that Tommy's parents fought most of the night and Tommy had no chance to study. He also knows that Tommy's father will give Tommy a beating if he finds out that he did poorly on the test. Jimmy wants to help Tommy, not himself, and shows Tommy some of the test answers. The teacher sees him. Should she reward Jimmy for cooperation and humanitarianism? Will she? Many of you will probably say that the teacher will not and should not reward Jimmy, for he cheated. Our immediate concern is not whether or not academic cheating is acceptable, but the point we are making is that the attitude promoted is that cooperation is less important than performing individualistically (might one say selfishly?) when tests and grades are involved.

Schools indoctrinate students to believe that problem solving is a solitary and highly individualized process, consisting of reading about the problem, discussing it with an authority—usually the teacher, and then writing about it in the form of a term paper or examination. In short, the student is taught that important questions are asked by authorities external to himself, that the answers to such questions are already known by those in authority, and that the way to solve such problems is to go to appropriate sources and find the predetermined answers. In the language of those outside of schools, this approach is negatively called "finding the textbook answer." Those outside schools know that they must identify for themselves most of the serious problems they face, and that there is not likely to be a predetermined solution to the problem that can be easily applied. They also know that many different people's ideas can be valuable, but that their solution will be their own and as such must be a reflection of their judgment. Evaluation of their efforts must also be done by themselves, even though others will also judge their actions. In other words, outside of school the way to solve a problem is not to read about it and then to write a formal examination paper.

A newly appointed principal with an excellent university record was faced with several problems in his school. His immediate response, a response that reflected the indoctrination he had received in his formal education, was to refer to his class notes and textbooks—the very materials that helped him achieve good grades as a student. Much to his chagrin, these sources didn't seem to offer any appropriate solution, and the teachers thought him rather naive in his assumption that authorities in educational administration had much to offer toward the solution of the problems at hand. Fortunately, the principal realized that though some help could be obtained from his formal training, there were many possible solutions, all of which had some merit, and therefore no predetermined good answer existed.

Thus far we have defined indoctrination, indicated how schools indoctrinate students, and spelled out the particular beliefs that students are expected to accept unquestioningly. We now move to the subject of *why* schools indoctrinate students. The first reason is simply that parents expect schools to inculcate in the young the norms of society. One has but to reflect briefly to know that there has never been a society that supported an individual or group that wanted to overthrow it. Our society is not likely to provide extensive support for schools without the assurance that schools are teaching students to accept society's economic, political, and social values.

School officials, such as teachers and administrators, represent in large measure those in society who are dedicated to maintaining the basic aspects of the status quo, for they have typically been selected and rewarded for behavior consistent with this value orientation. They are, in other words, trustworthy and proper persons to relate to young impressionable minds.

Adults in critical decision-making positions in society consider it essential that the young accept those basic values that underline the directions that society has chosen to take. Students, for example, must believe that a continuing development of technology is good (the more the better) or else they might choose to reject such beliefs (much as many young people have done in recent years). The overreaction of many adults to the youthful phenomenon of dropping out gives credibility to the view that adults are threatened by those, especially the young, who don't accept their values. (If young people had chosen to swallow goldfish or stuff themselves in phone booths, this would have been considered fanciful rather than threatening behavior for it would not strike at the core of adult belief systems.)

Indoctrination is inevitable in schools and colleges, but we question the degree of emphasis on it and manner in which it occurs. This matter of extent and manner is not fully explained by societal expectations and demands, so we must look further for an explanation.

The incipient scholar or successful student model has its own assumptions which must be accepted by students or else activities carried on by educators would be subject to constant challenge, if not open rebellion. These assumptions are that

(1) Schools exist in order to educate students;

(2) What schools do is education;

(3) To be educated, one must succeed in schools, and those who don't succeed in schools are by definition not educated.

Ironically, most students accept these assumptions without question in spite of the fact that many school practices make little or no sense to many, if not most, of the students.

The actual model that schools follow and the assumptions that are the basis for this model are:

(1) Schools exist to produce successful students or incipient scholars;

(2) Schools have students do those things that incipient scholars do, and reward and sanction accordingly;

(3) To be a successful student, one must succeed in school.

At this point you might well ask what are the alternatives to the present degree of emphasis given to indoctrination, the content or subject matter of such indoctrination, and the manner in which the indoctrination is imposed on students? First, let us make it clear that the successful student model is of *pragmatic* value to many students, and these students can "profit" from acquiring the skills and attitudes necessary to continued academic success. Yet they should seriously question the model's appropriateness for development of such personal qualities as humanitarianism, sociability, and self-fulfillment. On the other hand, there is a large group of students, particularly those who will not continue their formal schooling beyond high school graduation, for whom the successful student model is of questionable value. Schools fail to meet these students' personal needs and interests and also fail to teach them useful knowledge and skills. For example, the student's study of government, consistent with the incipient scholar model, focuses on the three branches of government and involves memorization and recall of a body of facts. It fails to communicate how government and government officials behave. The student fails doubly for he not only learns an inaccurate view of the real political process, but also fails to learn how he can personally participate in the political process.

Neither the successful student nor the unsuccessful student learn about reality outside the school. At least we can say that they fail on the basis of most classroom instruction. The student government officer is taught that government officials operate in a highly structured, antiseptic manner, and the unsuccessful student's instruction also misses the mark.

What are some of the ways in which the student would learn in a model different from the incipient scholar model? For illustrative purposes, we have chosen to describe some of the activities the student would participate in if he were part of "the citizen participation model." He would, for example,

(1) Become involved in simulated political situations as an active participant;

(2) Interact with political officials;

(3) Observe political activities inside and outside the school;

(4) Actively participate in political activities inside and outside the school.

This approach is less prescriptive, more individualized, less subject to quantitative evaluation; hence it does not lend itself to bureaucratic model schools as they presently exist. It does, however, seem quite appropriate for the professional model that we advocate for curriculum and instruction and discuss in chapters 3 and 4. (We will discuss alternative models at greater length in the concluding section of this chapter.)

Sorting

As decision-makers, we use classification all the time. To classify phenomena according to particular criteria makes it much easier to live predictably. All winter clothing and raincoats are hung in the hallway closet, all mother's clothing is hung in her closet or placed in her dresser, and similar kinds of classification also determine where other members of the family put their clothing. Classification is so important in our lives that S. I. Hayakawa says that "Most intellectual problems are, ultimately, problems of classification and nomenclature."[5]

What is important to note is the power the classifier has if he can get others to accept his system of classification. For groups and societies regard as true "those systems of classification that produce the desired results."[6] Is organized baseball a business or a profession? Is aspirin a drug or not? Is a person whose ancestry is 10 percent black and 90 percent white a Negro or a Caucasian? In answering such questions various interest groups use classification to promote their views.

Sorting, as the term is used in this book, is the process one goes through to implement one's classification system. (Sorting can occur at random without using a system of classification as its rationale. The teacher, for example, might say, "Ten of you join this group and ten of you join that group.") Sorting allows the decision-maker to pursue his objectives in a systematic and predictable manner. As such, it is a powerful tool in the hands of the persons who use it.

We have argued that the primary operational objective of the schools is the production of incipient scholars or successful students. Sorting thus becomes an important function that aids the school in producing incipient scholars. A major sorting criterion is grades—the currency of the schools. The student who receives good grades is rewarded with special privileges, such as the opportunity to serve in the student government, eligibility for special courses, clubs, and committees, and entrance into the college preparatory program and into college itself. One of the main rewards gained by those who get good grades is the general approbation of teachers and administrators—people who believe that good grades are important to assure success in formal education.

In the elementary grades, students are usually sorted by reading ability. Although reading groups frequently have innocuous titles such as bluebirds, canaries, and robins, the children soon learn that the titles mean one, two, and three, or fast, average, and slow. (This raises the question as to why other criteria, e.g., social maturity, are not used for sorting purposes.) Elementary school students are also sorted according to standardized tests, such as I.Q. tests. The results of these tests become very important to some teachers and parents who know how to tap the school grapevine. The slightest glimmer of hope sends many parents into ecstacy, for they feel their child has demonstrated he or she is college material.

During the student's junior high school or middle school years, he is often sorted according to academic grades, although most sorting is done on the basis of his projected potential to pursue a college preparatory course in high school. If he has academic success as a junior high or middle school student and his parents have high expectations, he will be placed in the college preparatory program (advanced or regular) at the end of junior high school or middle school. If he is not considered to be college material he will be placed in another, less prestigious track such as the general course of study or the vocational program. Programs below the college preparatory level water down the regular academic subjects, which if undiluted help assure the high school student of entrance to if not success in colleges and universities.[7]

The self-image of the student is highly affected by sorting in our schools. A student who is not rewarded by the incipient scholar mode often learns to think of himself as a "dummy." (He was a robin in reading, a low scorer on standardized tests, a recipient of Cs and Ds in most academic subjects, and was placed in the vocational education track.)

The successful student learns to conform to school rules and regulations, and is generally considered to have made the adjustment to school. This means that schools classify students into two gross categories: successful students, and the others.

One of the main goals of those who classify and sort is to get others to accept these functions as legitimate. Students are taught to accept sorting as a legitimate function of schools. It is relatively easy to see how students and their parents who are rewarded by the sorting process in schools would accept the way sorting occurs, but what about the students and parents who are not rewarded by the sorting procedures used in schools? How can the C or D student and his parents be pacified? This matter is especially critical and controversial for the beginning high school student and his parents. If the student does not perform well, as evidenced by grades and high standardized test scores, he and his parents must be convinced that he is not an incipient scholar or college material, and that this is okay. One of the main ways in which this legitimizing function takes place is by teaching students and parents to believe that the incipient scholar model is also the model employed in the larger society outside the school. The rhetoric is consistent with the philosophy of social Darwinism: "In school as anywhere in life you have to be tough—the cream rises to the top—and those who don't simply haven't put themselves into it."

Those who are sorted out rather than sorted in are also taught that different people have different interests and everyone does something well. "It just so happens that Johnny likes marbles rather than textbooks. Johnny will do well somewhere even though he isn't a successful student." (We're not quite sure if Johnny is headed for a marble championship or an assembly line worker's job in a marble factory.)

Why does sorting occur the way it does in our schools? The first reason is that it reflects societal expectations and demands. Technological advances in our nation have meant that longer and longer periods of training are necessary, and means that decisions must be made earlier and earlier as to who will most likely succeed in advanced training such as medical school or law school. In order for society to have the kind of labor or vocational assignment it needs, the schools have been charged with sorting out the students. The matter can't be left to chance.

Secondly, the bureaucratic instructional organizations known as schools require sorting in order to fulfill their own vision as to what instruction should be. Grades, standardized test scores, citizenship marks, and the like give members of the school as a sociopolitical system *tangible* evidence about the progress of students. Schools can operate in a systematic and predictable manner, which lends security to their members. Teachers can behave much as they were taught to behave. Sorting also means that all students in a particular class or category will move along at the same pace, thus making their progress much easier to evaluate. (Teachers who really try to evaluate a student on the basis of his progress from the time he enters the class to the time he leaves it—without comparison to others in the class—are subject to a good deal of criticism, especially from colleagues.)

There are several alternatives to the present model for sorting that exists in our schools. As with other functions, we disagree with both the level of intensity and manner in which sorting occurs; at the same time, we believe that it is impossible to eliminate sorting in any organization, including the schools.

Some subjects in schools may demand more rigid sorting practices than others. For example, many foreign language teachers argue that French I should precede French II and Spanish I should precede Spanish II. (Some language teachers argue that a teacher and his students should study a language, such as Swahili, that is unknown to both teacher and students, for the important thing is to know how to learn a language rather than learning a *particular* language.) However, most sorting practices are arbitrary and largely for the convenience of the sorter rather than the instruction of the child. A professor of science education estimates that a motivated twelve-year-old of average intelligence can by intensive application learn basic science skills and concepts in six weeks, as evidenced in an average score or higher on science achievement tests for his grade level. Presently the twelve-year-old child has spent four hours a week for four years learning the same basic concepts and skills. Many students have been sorted out in the process and their self-images affected in a negative way.

Schools should also consider criteria other than those presently used for sorting purposes. If, for example, pluralism and ethnicity are valued as positive learnings in social studies, why not consider these in sorting? White students might well take courses in black dialect rather than or in addition to Latin and French. Interdisciplinary cooperation might be effected by organizing and sorting students according to their interest in subjects such as environmental education and race relations. This would call for a variety of instructional techniques and evaluation procedures. If the professional model for curriculum and instruction prevailed, rather than the bureaucratic model, the professional judgments of teachers would be the basis for new criteria for sorting.

Providing the Conditions for Personal Development

Educational rhetoric promises the student the opportunity to examine who he presently is in relation to what he would like to become. Furthermore, schools claim that they create the conditions whereby the student will be aided in this creative process. These promises are philosophical, for they claim to establish the conditions for introspection and reorientation of personal beliefs.

It is not by accident that we have placed "providing the conditions for personal or self-development" last on our list of functions performed by schools. This function is, in our judgment, treated incidentally, accidentally, and in an ancillary way by schools in spite of its prominence in lists of *stated* goals. Confining, training, indoctrinating, and sorting are easily measured technical functions consistent with a bureaucratic organization's basic assumptions. They are clearly consistent with the school's interest in producing *successful* students. The student who demonstrates that he performs these four functions well and in the process accepts the functions as legitimate will be rewarded with the currency of the school: good grades.

On the other hand, the student who seriously pursues the more philosophical matter of knowing himself and what he wants to become will find this function working against him *unless* he accepts and performs well the first four functions. The instructional reward system is not adjusted to the student who gives top priority to the fifth function. This means that the conditions for personal or self-development are established largely through the idiosyncratic efforts of individual teachers, administrators, and staff members (teacher aides and other paraprofessionals). One major way in which this is done is in extracurricular activities such as athletics, social clubs, and quasi academic organizations, which are designed to reach the student's total gestalt—physical, emotional, and cognitive. Social sensitivity and cooperation, for example, are part of the operational objectives of many of these extracurricular activities. In the following essay, a high school student expresses what an extracurricular activity, a government and economics seminar, meant to her compared to the more formal classroom atmosphere in which most instruction takes place:

To most American high school students, words such as economic determinism, epistemology, utilitarianism, altruism, and humanism are unfamiliar. They are terms students may have come across in their reading and have not bothered to search for in the dictionary. However, it is during these years of high school when many young people are experiencing an "awakening," a sharpening of their powers of curiosity, judgment, and analysis, that they are particularly receptive to learning the significance of terms and concepts. With an increasing awareness of themselves as individuals possessing the ability to accept or reject, condemn or condone the myriad solutions to the problems confronting man, students are anxious to explore, partly out of curiosity but also to develop their own personalities.

Herein lies the outstanding value of a program such as senior seminars, wherein the works of a wide variety of reputable authors are read and ample opportunity to discuss the ideas is afforded.

The seminars that I attended were meaningful to me and to many of my classmates for reasons I've already indicated. Usually held in homes of students, the seminars were characterized by a relaxed, friendly atmosphere. It was not uncommon to find 50 or 60 persons crowded in a basement "rec" room. All of them came to learn something, not just to visit with their friends.

At the outset of each evening, the role of the teacher was important for he often initiated the discussion by throwing out a challenging question or asking if anyone in the group had a particular point that he wanted discussed. It was also his function, if students wandered off on too many irrelevant tangents, to steer them back to the original topic. Sometimes, though, one question would lead to another, and the original theme of the discussion would be forgotten.

One evening when we were discussing various economic theories, someone brought up altruism, which subsequently generated a heated debate concerning the connection between altruism and religion. Because the topic was of interest to the majority, the teacher did not curtail further discussion. Instead of inhibiting students by exercising too much control over the discussion or by advancing too many of his own views, the teacher was able to promote an atmosphere conducive to productive thinking. Those who felt like arguing could express themselves freely, while those who came just to listen did not feel uncomfortable. Many students felt the discussions were solely for listening to.

Students of high school age are concerned with many of the problems confronting society, but often, because of a lack of understanding, or a feeling of immaturity, are embarrassed to express their concern in a classroom situation. However, in an informal situation such as that afforded by senior seminars, where interested students come together for the specific purpose of discussing subjects of this nature, the problem of self-consciousness is minimized.

It is extremely valuable to have an interested and sympathetic adult listen to and comment on one's views and to have an opportunity to question and comment on the views of one another.[8]

One of the main conditions for personal development is an option, if the student wishes to use it, for privacy. The student must have the opportunity to be alone much more than he is in today's schools. Schools are so regimented that every working moment of the school day is consumed by normal classroom activities. This explains one of the reasons for the difficulty college preparatory students have in adjusting during their first year in college: students who have just graduated from high school are not used to free time.

Given the disparity between public school rhetoric about the conditions for personal development and the reality, why is this function included in the rhetoric? First, good public relations requires that this function be part of the rhetoric, for parents expect schools to do more than turn out successful students or incipient scholars. Many if not most parents have a realistic memory, if sometimes romantic, of their own involvement in extracurricular activities when they were students. Those parents who went on to higher education realize the pragmatic value of good grades while still acknowledging the importance of extracurricular activities. Other parents look back to their days in school as beneficial primarily because of their involvement in extracurricular activities. For these reasons and others, school administrators know the importance of including self-fulfilling objectives in public relations literature and speeches.

It is also true that tension among students, teachers, and staff is often minimized due to rhetoric and action for self-fulfillment. To some extent this is accomplished by a trade-off: students are told to work hard on their subjects and then they will be given something they really want.

Finally, there are many teachers who believe that providing conditions for personal development is a basic part of their role, and they act accordingly.

Although we have criticized schools for failing to provide adequate conditions for self-development, the reader might well ask, "What alternatives are there to the situation as it presently exists?" Schools should provide for more formal recognition of the value of activities that do not support present conceptions of the successful student. The concept of the student as an incipient scholar is too narrow, and tends to exclude more important conceptions. The student who described her experience in a senior seminar demonstrated the importance of the teacher's approbation in saying that "It is extremely valuable to have an interested and sympathetic adult listen to and comment on one's views and to have an opportunity to question and comment on the views of one another." Both informal and formal ways of rewarding students who value the function of personal development can be used if the school really believes the function is important. At the present, however, schools act as if this function is of minimal importance compared with the other four.

If the teacher has as his model the university professor he will probably not emphasize the fifth function as much as he should, and if he has a bureaucratic orientation he also will probably not emphasize this function for it would make his job more complex. (Grading, for example, would be much more difficult.) The teacher who supports the professional model much as we have defined it will recognize that he must individualize school activities to serve his clients—the students.

If providing the conditions for self-development is given higher priority in schools, administrators will have to define a new role for themselves. They will largely be political rather than instructional leaders, they will be bureaucrats who for the most part leave curriculum and instruction to the professionals (teachers). Their new role will largely consist of interpreting to public and legal bodies less traditional and less familiar approaches to curriculum and instruction. Instead of spending 80 percent of their time in school and 20 percent of their time outside the school, they will spend 80 percent of their time outside and 20 percent of their time in school. Increased public interest in issues such as environmental education, drug education, and race relations will lend support to such a role reversal.

Conclusion

In this chapter we have identified and described five functions that educational organizations perform for students: confinement, training, indoctrination, sorting, and providing the conditions for personal or self-development. The first four functions are taken seriously by educational organizations and present practices are consistent with the bureaucratic model for organization. We have argued that the professional model for curriculum and instruction is more appropriate for the first four functions, and particularly for the fifth function: providing conditions for personal development of students. At the same time, we believe that all five functions are provided in some measure by all organizations. However, the manner in which such functions are performed, including the degree of emphasis and timing, is critical and can be changed to create educational organizations that serve their students better.

Notes for Chapter 2

1. State laws typically charge school authorities with responsibility for the welfare of students while they are in attendance. This charge, however, does not explain or justify the rigidity with which many schools confine students to meet this legal requirement.

2. The principal of one school expressed his disagreement with this tendency by saying, "I will not deal with the behavior of 10 percent of our students by restricting the behavior of all of them for two reasons: idealistic and pragmatic. Idealistically it's simply unjust, and pragmatically the most effective way to deal with the 10 percent is on an individual basis. General rules are likely to stir up the majority of students." This was put even more succinctly by the headmaster of a prestigious Eastern school who used to tell each new student, "There are no rules here but if you break any you're in trouble."

3. Ivan Illich clearly demonstrates this in *Deschooling Society* (New York: Harper & Row, 1971): "School sells curriculum—a bundle of goods made according to the same process and having the same structure as merchandise" (page 41). Illich criticizes university graduates, who naturally reflect the university's role as consumers, and he argues that growth as open-ended consumption can't lead to maturity, which is organic development (page 43).

4. Theodore Brameld, "What is Indoctrination?" *School and Society* 85 (Nov. 9, 1957): 326. It should be noted that the word *indoctrination* is translated from the original Italian (indottrinaire) and French (endoctriner) as "to imbue with learning, to teach." The *Oxford English Dictionary* (Oxford, England: The Clarendon Press, 1933), vol. 5, p. 226. The commonly accepted negative connotation of the word in the United States is an exception to its usage both historically and in many parts of the world today.

5. S. I. Hayakawa, *Language in Thought and Action* (New York: Harcourt, Brace and World, 1964), p. 220.

6. Ibid., p. 223.

7. In one school system, probably representative of many others, eighth grade students took the following message home to their parents in April: "My counselors said that I need to choose Latin or French if I want to go to college." Students were also advised to take algebra rather than general math for the same reason.

8. Dale L. Brubaker and Georgia Turner, "A New Teacher Seeks a Catalyst," *Michigan Education Journal* (May 1966): 15, 42.

(3)

The School as a Bureaucratic Organization

In the previous chapter, the five functions performed by schools were discussed. There were several references to the fact that schools and colleges are organized bureaucratically for performance of their instructional functions. We now turn to a discussion of how and why schools are organized bureaucratically, pointing out that though a bureaucratic structure seems to make sense for governance in educational organizations, it does not seem the most effective way to organize for instruction. This chapter compares the bureaucratic organizational model with the professional organizational model, and proposes a new organizational model from which schools might well profit.

This discussion of the bureaucratic model for instruction should help the reader understand better the parameters which limit or are designed to limit the decisions he can make. Consequently, this chapter provides much of the information that will enable the reader to make a realistic assessment of the organization in which he works and hence enable him to utilize effectively those concepts and guides to action which make up Part 2 of this book.

Although you, the reader, have been a member of several bureaucracies since birth and will be until death, you have probably not studied bureaucracies, including the school, in a systematic manner. Whether you are basically satisfied with schools as they are and advocate only minor changes, or whether you think that radical changes are needed in our schools, it is to your advantage to know how schools operate.

Schools as Governmental Organizations

Part of the folklore about schools is the belief that they are primarily concerned with meeting the needs of their clients, the students. We often hear that students should, as a result of their schooling, develop to their full potential, recognize their own worth as individuals, and become productive citizens in a democracy. In fact, this is a half-truth. It is true to the extent that the school as a bureaucracy tries to meet students' needs within a predetermined and larger context—a context with its own value commitments, techniques for reaching such commitments, and evaluative procedures that indicate whether or not such commitments are being reached.

We have identified this larger context as the governmental context. That is, we can best understand the school and its operations if we view the school as a governmental operation. The schools are designed to implement the objectives of state, local, and federal governments, and as such are an expression of these governments. The three governing bodies provide the financial support for school and for all practical purposes designate how, when, and where the money will and will not be spent. Governmental bodies decide how many days school will be open each year, what subjects will be taught, and who is qualified to teach. The governmental bodies interested in formal education control both the entrance and exit of members of the school as a sociopolitical system, and influence the quality of existence between the entrance and exit points. Though teachers and other school personnel may influence such decisions, final authority always rests with one of the three governmental bodies—local, state, or federal.

A first year teacher who is concerned with the needs of students has already had her role prescribed by two governmental bodies. University preparation of teachers is influenced by governmental bodies. The prospective teacher's certification is granted by the state, which has prescribed a course of study for the future teacher. If a prospective teacher needs financial support while studying at the university, the federal government may lend such support.

The teaching situation in the first year teacher's school is even more rigidly prescribed by local, state, and federal governments. For example, the following are some of the things that have been decided for the teacher:

(1) The minimum number of days, hours, and minutes she will spend with students, regardless of each student's individual needs and desires (state government influence);

(2) The subjects to be taught (mainly state government influence);

(3) Most of the "approved" teaching materials, such as textbooks (state and local government influence);

(4) The way student progress or lack of progress is to be reported (local government influence); and

(5) The curriculum (state and local government influence).

It is true that there are some variations as to how our first year teacher can meet the individual needs of students, but time, place, and to a large extent the means for meeting students' needs have already been prescribed by governmental acts.

As a decision-maker, the reader might at this point say, "So what? I already knew that governments influenced schools." The most important point is that "the great distinction between government and other organized undertaking is to be found in the wholly political character of government."[1] The political character of government dictates that a particular decision is the result of a political evaluation *anticipating popular reaction.* The level in the organization at which a decision is made is determined by an evaluation of the degree of controversy the decision is likely to generate. The overriding variable in the decision will be the assessment of public reaction to it, rather than its efficacy or soundness from an education standpoint. The following example illustrates this principle:

A senior English teacher, after assessing the needs of her students and the availability of current novels appropriate to those needs and interests, decides to assign *Catcher in the Rye.* Her colleagues in the English department fully concur in her selection, but many of the students' parents are upset with language in the book and protest to school authorities, including the local school board. The school board rules that since there are many other books dealing with the life of an adolescent–books less likely to disturb the public–*Catcher in the Rye* is not the best selection for required reading in the English class.

This example clearly demonstrates the extent to which schools are influenced by public reaction and how decisions about curriculum are much more than educational decisions made by professionally qualified educators. Such decisions are always viewed politically by the school board, which is immediately subject to public reaction because it is an elected body. Those who fail to reckon with the political nature of decision-making in schools run the risk of being both politically and educationally ineffective.

In this example the level of controversy was contained within the community and the decision was made by a local government–the school board. In many decisions directly affecting the school curriculum and instruction the level of controversy is wider in scope, touching the state as well as local governments. The following example focuses on state government:

Because of campus unrest and the apparent rebellion of many youth as reflected in experimentation with drugs, dress styles, and long hair, legislators in the state of California were bombarded with letters from their constituents about the morality of youth in the state. Congressmen and others made political hay out of this interest and passed legislation about the schools' responsibility for teaching manners and morals:

> Each teacher shall endeavor to impress upon the minds of the pupils the principles of morality, truth, justice, patriotism, and a true comprehension of the rights, duties, and dignity of American citizenship, to teach them to avoid idleness, profanity, and falsehood, and to instruct them in manners and morals and the principles of a free government.[2]

Principals in California were required to sign affidavits saying that instruction in manners and morals occurred in their schools.

This decision by the California legislature demonstrates that the manners and morals problem was viewed by the public to be of such consequence that it could not be effectively handled at the local level alone. The essentially political nature of the decision as opposed to the purposes of education is indicated in the immediate charge to the schools to deal with the manners and morals problems among youth. Professional educators were not the primary group involved in this decision. They were likewise not the group who decided that this was a legitimate function of the school as compared to other social agencies, that this was a top priority matter compared to other priorities in the school curriculum, or whether teachers were qualified for such instruction. (A construction crew, for example, might be better prepared to teach youth to avoid idleness.) Drivers' training courses, home economics courses, and drug abuse courses serve as other examples of issues that state legislatures have directed schools to include in the curriculum.

The federal government is also actively involved in decisions that affect education in the schools. Most recently the federal government has exhibited much concern over bussing children out of their neighborhoods to balance ethnic compositions. From an educational standpoint, there is little evidence to indicate whether good or ill results from bussing.[3] Bussing, however, is a volatile national political issue and both Congress and the president seem determined to act on the basis of their perceptions of public reaction. Thus the decision is taken out of the hands of educators and their role becomes one of reacting to governmental legislation.

In sum:

(1) Decisions in governmental organizations such as schools are political decisions, that is, decisions are structured by preassessment of public reaction;

(2) The anticipated public reaction determines the level at which a decision is made: the more intense the reaction is projected to be, the higher the level at which the decision will be made, and conversely; and

(3) The kind and quality of decisions made by governmental

organizations are influenced primarily by anticipated public reaction rather than by their educational quality or soundness.[4]

Bureaucratic and Professional Organizational Models and Their Appropriateness for Governance, Curriculum and Instruction in Schools

Thus far we have demonstrated that the objectives for our schools and the functions they are expected to perform are primarily determined by political forces in the form of local, state, and federal governments. As form follows function, we now describe the particular form of organization that our schools take, which we have identified as bureaucracy.

The Bureaucratic Organizational Model

It is little wonder that schools are primarily organized as bureaucracies, for bureaucratic organization seems to be the most effective way of carrying out the functions of government.[5]

The term "bureaucracy" has a negative connotation to most people, for they equate it with endless red tape, gross inefficiency, administrative inflexibility, dehumanization, and a host of other equally unattractive characteristics. But to the social scientist,[6] bureaucracy is one means of organizing human activity, a type of formal organization with the following characteristics:

(1) The detailed subdivision of labor, to be performed by many different highly trained specialists;

(2) General rules and regulations to ensure objective and impersonal treatment of the organization's clients, and to coordinate the efforts of the organization's specialist workers to promote an orderly, systematic, and rational means of providing services; and

(3) Hierarchical relationships designed to ensure the coordination of the specialists' efforts by providing clear and rational allocation of authority and responsibility.[7]

Why are schools organized bureaucratically? The first reason is that bureaucracy provides for disciplined compliance with rules, regulations, and directives from superiors. There is no need for discourse about who has the authority to make decisions and direct the activities of others. The superintendent clearly has the legal authority to direct the activities of the principal, the principal has the legal authority to direct the activities of the teachers, and the teachers clearly have the legal authority to direct the activities of the students.

Secondly, the hierarchical organization of a bureaucracy provides clear lines of authority and responsibility so that individuals can readily be held accountable for their actions. In any organization primarily concerned with public reaction, fixing responsibility appears to be essential. Somebody's "head has to roll" when things go wrong.

A third reason is that bureaucracy seems best suited to organizations whose ends are discreet and measurable, whose objectives are clear and generally agreed on, and whose causal relationships between means and ends are readily demonstrable.[8] At the risk of oversimplification, the end of those who hold power in government is to maintain their power, the means to maintain that power is favorable public reaction to governmental acts, and the causal relationship between means and ends is obvious: you don't stay in power long if the people don't approve of what you are doing.

But does this really apply to schools as governmental organizations? Do we really have agreement on objectives for the schools? Do we know the means to use to achieve such objectives if they are agreed on? In other words, do we know what is good education for a particular child and do we know how to achieve it?

To answer these questions, we need to make a distinction between *governance* and *curriculum and instruction.* Governance encompasses (and translates) the formal, legal rules and regulations that control the overall operation of the organization. Governance decisions provide a framework in which daily decisions are made. Curriculum and instruction refers to that area within the school as a sociopolitical system where learning experiences for students occur. For our purposes we are not making fine distinctions between curriculum and instruction, although we recognize that such distinctions exist. We have outlined some of the decisions that fall into each of the categories:

Governance	*Curriculum and Instruction*
Rules concerning health and safety in the school.	The choice of course titles and content for such courses.
Directives concerning the maintenance of buildings.	Sequence and scope of the curriculum.
The decision to initiate a bond issue and particular issues to be voted on.	Choice of textbooks and other instructional materials.
Particular accounting procedures for the receipt and dispersal of funds.	The establishment of seminars for honor students.
The formation of committees designed to maintain a working structure for the year.	The decision to adopt team teaching as an alternative in ninth grade English.

Governance is appropriately a function of a bureaucratic organization. When the primary concern of the organization is public reaction, bureaucracy provides the appropriate structure for dealing with such reaction, for in it disciplined compliance, hierarchical arrangements, and a causal relationship between means and ends all exist.

If we are to judge the appropriateness of the bureaucratic model for schools by their stated goals, it is obvious that such a model falls short for curriculum and instruction and in fact for the educational process itself. Commonly cited educational goals include effective citizenship, command of the fundamental processes, worthy home membership, productive use of leisure time, development of ethical character, and the promotion of good health.[9] It should be apparent that these general, abstract goals are not most appropriately or efficiently carried out under the bureaucratic model. Keeping in mind the characteristics of a bureaucracy, with such goals:

(1) The ends are not discretely measurable due to the abstractness of the objectives;

(2) The means for reaching the goals are not agreed on; and

(3) The causal relationship between means and ends is not readily or concretely demonstrable.

As Blau and Scott indicate, "When the overall responsibility of the organization cannot be broken down into fairly routine specialized tasks . . . [such as] research, care of the ill, case work services, expert judgments of professionals rather than disciplined compliance with the commands of superiors must govern operations in the interest of efficiency."[10] Tasks designed to meet the general educational objectives of "worthy home membership" and effective citizenship cannot be broken down into routine, specialized tasks. Professional judgment rather than disciplined compliance with orders from superiors is the appropriate pattern for reaching such goals. If these goals are the ones schools actually hope to reach, the bureaucratic model is both inefficient and ineffective.

But it remains true that schools do employ the bureaucratic model for instruction and development of curriculum as well as for governance. The ultimate judges of what good instruction is or what curriculum should be are the chief administrators in the school system rather than the teachers.[11] Chief administrators control the reward and sanction system for the most part.

Let us now examine the actual goals for schools as determined by the operation of schools. According to the Educational Policies Commission of the National Education Association and the American Association of School Administrators, "There is a unique, central role for the rational powers of an individual, however, for upon them depends his ability to achieve his personal goals and to fulfill his obligations to society."[12] The natural extension of this central role for education is for the school to produce successful students. Successful students are easily measured, for they score high on standardized tests and they conform to school rules and regulations. In other words, they learn to behave well in the role of student.

The bureaucratic model is appropriate for schools when they have as their primary goal the production of incipient scholars, for the end is measurable (the production of successful students), the means are known (teach courses so that students can successfully complete examinations and standardized tests), and causation is known since only students who take courses and do well on examinations are successful students.

In summary, the bureaucratic model is best suited for curriculum and instruction if the overriding goal of the schools is to produce the professional student. However, schools claim that their goals are much broader than this, and in our judgment they should be. This raises the question as to what model is appropriate for meeting those goals that go beyond producing incipient scholars. What model would be inclusive enough to support such statements of generalized intent as the following cited by well-known curriculum theorist James B. Macdonald:

Schools should foster the development of human beings so that they

(1) are committed to the value and worth of each and every human being—as the central value of existence,

(2) are aware of potentiality which lies within themselves, and the social, intellectual, physical, and emotional possibilities of their environment for furthering and creating potentiality, and

(3) are aware of the possibility of transcending their present personal and social situations and are skilled in the processes of seeking transcendence.[13]

The Professional Organizational Model

The professional organizational model is found in such organizations as hospitals and research institutes. Three characteristics differentiate the professional model from the bureaucratic model:

First, the professional organization is primarily concerned with the discovery or application of knowledge. Its basic functions cannot be programmed and therefore cannot be carried out efficiently by hierarchical arrangement and compliance with administrative orders.

Secondly, professional organizations have many nonprofessional and semiprofessional workers who may be organized in the traditional bureaucratic manner, but basic decisions about functions are made by the professionals themselves.

Thirdly, professional organizations emphasize achievement of objectives rather than disciplined compliance to a highly programmed process for achieving objectives. Processes used in professional organizations can be highly flexible and individualistic as the professionals' judgment dictates.

The critical distinctions between the professional and bureaucratic models can be seen more clearly side by side:

Bureaucratic Model[14]	*Professional Model*[14]
The bureaucrat's foremost responsibility is to represent and promote the interests of his organization.	The professional is bound by a norm of service and a code of ethics to represent the welfare of his clients.
The bureaucrat gets his authority from a legal contract backed by the rights and privileges of his office.	The professional's source of authority comes from his technical competence and expertise and knowledge.
The bureaucrat's decisions are governed by disciplined compliance with directives from superiors.	The professional's decisions are governed by internalized professional standards.
The court of last resort for appeal of a decision by a bureaucrat is a higher management.	The court of last resort for appeal of a decision by a professional is his professional colleagues.

Let us now look at the difference it makes if a decision is made primarily according to the bureaucratic or professional model. We ask you, the decision-maker, to place yourself in the position of a visitor-inquirer in a school with which you are familiar. Check the column which indicates that a particular decision is made for the most part by a teacher's colleagues (the professional model) or the school administration, that is, supervisors, principals, superintendents (the bureaucratic model):

	Teachers	*Administrators*
(1) The qualifications for the assignment of teachers to a school. (Who should teach at what school?)	______	______
(2) The evaluation of a teacher's effectiveness as it relates to receiving tenure and getting salary increases.	______	______
(3) The decision as to which texts are to be used in the classroom.	______	______
(4) The decision that Johnny Jones would		

profit more from six weeks study in libraries and museums rather than in school. ______ ______

(5) The decision to experiment with giving no grades and having no report cards for one school term. ______ ______

(6) The decision the Jimmy Jackson should forgo reading groups for ten weeks since he has developed a negative attitude toward reading. ______ ______

(7) The decision to depart radically from the state curriculum guide for a group of seventh graders, for whom the guide in the judgment of the teacher seems totally inappropriate. ______ ______

(8) The decision to invite the chairman of the local Black Panther Party to address the students in an eighth grade class. ______ ______

(9) The decision as to whether or not a teacher has handled a discipline problem properly. ______ ______

(10) The decision as to whether or not a novel selected by a tenth grade English teacher is appropriate reading for the students. ______ ______

Schools vary as to the degrees of professionalism and bureaucratization they contain. It is our contention that most schools will lean more toward the bureaucratic model than the professional model (most of your checks were probably placed under administrators rather than teachers), which is to be expected since most schools are government organizations and are organized bureaucratically for instruction, since the primary objective is to produce "good" students or incipient scholars.

A New Organizational Model for Schools

We have noted that schools are primarily organized bureaucratically to respond appropriately to public reaction. However, we seriously questioned whether or not schools should be organized bureaucratically for curriculum and instruction if they are to to do more than meet the simplistic objective of producing good students. Our bias is obvious, for we believe that schools *should* do more. This section of the book proposes a new organizational model for schools that combines the professional and bureaucratic models, a combination necessary if schools are to do justice to their clients and meet the needs of the inner city, suburban, and rural child in our society.

First, let us recognize that bureaucracy cannot be eliminated from the schools, for it is a requisite of governmental organizations and schools are governmental organizations. But the bureaucratic model is patently inappropriate for meeting the needs of the diverse student population we have today. If schools are to achieve the objectives recommended by James B. Macdonald and others, the professional model is more appropriate than the bureaucratic model. We are in fact faced with an organizational dilemma that can only be reconciled or endured. An example of this dilemma on a personal plane is the young person whose religious beliefs differ radically from his parents' beliefs. He loves his parents and they love him. The close relationship with his parents is something he does not want to relinquish, yet he cannot subscribe to their religious beliefs and his parents cannot accept his. This dilemma cannot be resolved. It can, however, be reconciled if parents and son tacitly agree to avoid confrontation over religious beliefs and respect the privacy of each other's beliefs.

An example of reconciliation between the bureaucratic and professional models is found in public hospitals. The public hospital is dependent on the local and/or state, and/or federal governments for support, and is accountable to those governments for compliance with their rules and regulations. At the same time, the public hospital provides treatment for its patients within a model more professional than bureaucratic. The medical profession decides who can practice in the hospital, what treatments are appropriate for what patients, and the competence of their colleagues, the medical doctors. The nonprofessional staff of the hospital—nurses, technicians, and aides—are typically organized bureaucratically and are governed by professional decisions made by medical doctors.

The challenge to those in education is to reconcile the bureaucratic with the professional model in a manner similar to the way that the dilemma has been solved in public hospitals and other governmental organizations. Public reaction is the critical factor, since support of the organization is dependent on favorable public reaction. The professional organization decides first what is good practice and then convinces the public of the efficacy of that practice. The bureaucratic organization weighs public reaction first and then institutes those practices least likely to cause public furor. (No organization will fit perfectly either model but one mode of decision-making will tend to predominate. The model that does predominate will indicate whether the organization is primarily professional or bureaucratic.) It is our contention that schools tend to adopt the bureaucratic mode. For example, too often the superintendent attempts to influence instruction and curriculum so that they will meet the least resistance from the public rather than accepting the professional judgments of his teachers about the soundness of curriculum and instruction practices, after which he should prepare himself to meet adverse public reaction.

Professional Model	*Bureaucratic Model*
Make decision	Anticipate public reaction
Implement decision	Make decision
Deal with public reaction	Implement decision

The basic problem the professional faces in dealing with public reaction is that his relationship with his clients—those for whom he provides services—is a tenuous one since his clients often try to dictate to him how he should provide his professional services. The professional cannot permit his clients to dictate to him, except within well-defined limits, for to do so would be abdicating his professional responsibility to apply his expert knowledge. In public hospitals, which involve a marriage of the bureaucratic and professional models, the physicians are under pressure to cater to the whims of the patient and/or his family, but anyone who has spent any time in a hospital knows that doctors resist this pressure effectively. Doctors must be responsive to their clients as far as the general results of their services, such as curing disease and maintenance of health, but their patients cannot dictate how such services will be applied to reach these general ends.

The folklore of formal education claims that the clients, that is, students, parents, and citizens in general, are well qualified to decide the ends of education and the means to reach such ends. The school board is not only qualified to establish literacy as an objective for the schools, but also prescribes the means to achieve literacy, including the curriculum, the teaching staff, and instructional organization.

All this does not mean that students, parents, and citizens should not actively participate in establishing the objectives of the schools. It *does* mean that the means for reaching those objectives should primarily be the concern of professionals, the teachers, otherwise teachers will continue to play their present role as bureaucratic functionaries who are in effect midwives for public reaction.[15]

Conclusion

In this chapter we have made the following points: (1) schools are government organizations and consequently are organized bureaucratically; (2) as government organizations, schools must anticipate and deal effectively with public reaction; (3) the bureaucratic model is appropriate for the governance of schools but less than satisfactory for curriculum and instruction matters; (4) the professional model is more appropriate for the curriculum development and instructional aspect of school organization; and (5) what we need is a new model for our schools, a model that effects the marriage of the bureaucratic and professional models.

Notes for Chapter 3

1. Paul H. Appleby, *Policy and Administration* (University, Alabama: University of Alabama Press, 1949), p. 12.

2. *Education Code,* vol. 1 (Sacramento, California: State of California, 1963), p. 356.

3. The following alternatives, for example, may be educationally sounder but not politically viable: (1) triple the expenditures for pupils in inner city and distressed area rural schools and provide many special services appropriate to such pupils; (2) provide that no federal funds can be used for housing construction unless occupancy is based on a ratio consistent with the city's racial mix; and/or (3) implement a voucher plan whereby students may elect to attend any school of their choice.

4. The inconsistency of the federal government, particularly the United States Office of Education, with regard to plans and programs most deserving support serves as an example. Education for the gifted, creativity, integration, compensatory education, vocational education, the right to read, accountability, and behavioral objectives were catch-words of the last decade. It is little wonder that educationists are accused of faddism, for these terms reflect the fact that political winds blow from alternating directions with different intensity from year to year.

5. One might disagree with the effectiveness of bureaucracy as a form of government organization, but one cannot argue as to the universality of the bureaucratic model. All governmental organizations are organized bureaucratically.

6. See Max Weber et al., *The Theory of Social and Economic Organization* (New York: Oxford University Press, 1947).

7. Bertram M. Gross, *The Managing of Organizations* (Glencoe, Ill.: The Free Press of Glencoe, 1964), p. 49.

8. Peter M. Blau and W. Richard Scott, *Formal Organizations* (San Francisco: Chandler Publishing Company, 1962), pp. 206-210.

9. See for example "The Central Purpose of American Education," quoted in the *National Education Association Journal* (Sept. 1961).

10. Blau and Scott, *op. cit.*, p. 297.

11. Governing bodies and their representatives, the administrators, set the conditions or establish the basic environment for curriculum and instruction. They determine class size, student composition in classes, number of days of instruction, the schedule for such instruction, and who will teach.

12. *The Central Purpose of American Education, op. cit.*, p. 9.

13. James B. Macdonald, "The High School in Human Terms: Curriculum Design," in *Humanizing the Secondary School*, edited by Norman K. Hamilton and J. Galen Saylor (Washington, D.C.: Association for Supervision and Curriculum Development, 1969), p. 48.

14. Blau and Scott, *op. cit.*, p. 297.

15. Much of the literature in education promotes the idea that students should be full partners in planning for their instruction. This has especially been true of recent literature. Such participation is salutary for motivating students and for providing information about students to the teacher. But motivational techniques and collection of information about students should not be confused with educational decision-making.

(4)

Institutions of Higher Education as Bureaucratic Organizations

The following essays focus on curriculum and instruction in institutions of higher education. This is important to note, for institutions of higher education also have important research and service functions. In our discussion of elementary and secondary schools we observed that their primary goal is the production of incipient scholars. Institutions of higher education not only carry this theme forward but give it added emphasis. This is true in spite of rhetoric some people come to take at face value: "It is the aim of our university to help create thoughtful citizens who will take an active part in the life of the community and nation." This kind of rhetoric is at best ambiguous and at worst gratuitous. In short, such admirable goals are an incidental result of out-of-class activity; in-class activities are designed to produce the incipient scholar.

In the first section, "An Admission Man's Guide to College Organization," admissions in higher education is the main subject. Admissions is the vehicle that carries out the transition from schools to institutions of higher education. It is argued that the purposes of higher education structure the institution's goals and objectives.

The second section, "The University as an Institutional Bureaucracy," demonstrates how institutions of higher education are organized bureaucratically for curriculum and instruction in order to produce incipient scholars. As long as this is the goal of higher education we can expect the bureaucratic model to prevail.

An Admission Man's Guide to College Organization*

In his introduction to *The American College,* Nevitt Sanford succinctly phrased the difficulties inherent in any realistic and objective analysis of college organization. "Practice in higher education, as in politics, remains largely untouched by the facts and principles of science," he said. "What our colleges do tends either to be governed by tradition or to be improvised in the face of diverse—usually unanticipated—pressures. . . . Very little is known of what effects, if any, the experience of going to college has on students, and less on what particular features of the college environment determine such effects as have been observed."[1]

Sanford's comments about our knowledge of the practices of the college in general are even truer of our knowledge of the practices of the admissions officer in particular. The literature purporting to describe or prescribe the functions of the admissions officer is largely unsupported by empirical study, and where such study has been done it is largely of the status variety, uncritically describing current practices.

Agreement exists that the admissions officer has much to do with the admission of students, but answers to questions of how and for what purpose or purposes are not supported by substantive research or systematic theory. Rather, there is a plethora of prescription applicable perhaps to one or a few colleges but of little relevance to the admissions officer who must relate his day-to-day tasks to the practices of his college. A statement that the admissions officer's function is "to organize, coordinate, and guide the relationship of the faculty with prospective students without himself standing in the

* Reprinted, with permission, from *College Board Review* no. 61 (fall 1966): 14-20, College Entrance Examination Board, New York.

way," may have real meaning to the person who said it, but offers little help to the man who must decide what to organize for, for what purposes, what to coordinate, in what manner, and at what time.

Answers to such questions are not to be found in prescriptions, and particularly not in prescriptions which themselves are contradictory. For example, the article in the winter 1963 *College Board Review* that contained the above statement[2] also prescribed that the admissions officer should "become more closely involved with the students and faculty of his own institution. . . . His roots should again be firmly embedded in the campus soil." This article made a reasonable case for the admissions officer's curtailing his visits to schools and concentrating more on building a sound relationship with his own faculty. A later article in the fall 1963 *Review*[3] decried the breakdown in communications between the schools and the colleges in the area of admissions, and offered as a remedy more contact between school and college personnel—particularly the representatives of the admissions office. One might conclude that the dilemma could be resolved by the college admissions officer were he to stay on his campus more while visiting more high schools.

In fairness to the authors of the articles, it should be pointed out that each had a good case and each presented his case well. The dilemma their articles raised was not a result of their inaccurate assessment of some very real problems nor of the inappropriateness of the solutions they offered.

The dilemma posed for the admissions officer could be resolved only if the admissions officer were able to recognize the frames of reference of each author and the relevance of such frames of reference to his own situation. The admissions officer needs a theoretical framework, some working models of colleges in general and of his college in particular, if he is to view with perspective those prescriptions that tell him what—and what not—to do.

This section will develop such models. It will not prescribe.

Four models[4] of immediate relevance to the instructional function of the college are: (1) the teaching output model—the end result of the instructional processes of the college, the graduate; (2) the instructional organizational model, which determines how the faculty and other resources of the college will be utilized to produce that graduate; (3) the model of the college's needs, or the *ends* for which it exists; and (4) the model of the admissions officer as the regulator of student inputs.

How College Catalogs Mislead

The teaching output model cannot be constructed accurately from the descriptions in a college's catalog, which are usually generalized statements about the "educated man," and paint a picture of an idealized future state of human development. Only the recalcitrant will disagree with them; only the omniscient can measure them. Who could disagree with or measure attainment by using the following statement from a current university bulletin:

> An educated man will acquire at least some experience in the three divisions of human knowledge and inquiry; the world of nature—the physical and life sciences; the world of man in relation to man—the social sciences; the world of spirit and imagination—the humanities.
>
> The objective is a man capable of thinking in the markedly different ways represented by these three divisions; for each of them he will familiarize himself with the appropriate method and idiom as well as the particular purpose and scope. . . . In short, a liberal education should help a man to know, to understand, to decide, and to express: to know the facts or how to find them, to understand those facts with insight and perspective, to decide only after understanding and conscious evaluation, and to express those decisions with ease and grace.

Such statements have a noble ring; they appeal to the best in us all. But they are much too subjective, much too idealized, to serve as useful output descriptions. How do you measure these abilities in a student? Obviously you can't. Then how do you determine the true output objectives of the college's instruction? Look to its graduation requirements: in the above case, 122 semester hours' credit with a minimum grade-point average, hours to be distributed among courses in general education (the three divisions of human knowledge and inquiry), a major in one discipline, courses related to the major, and elective courses.

The college's graduation requirements describe its real output objectives: a person who can complete a set of prescribed courses, completion to be measured by devices such as examinations, term papers, and class recitation and to be attested to by professors assigned to teach one or more of the prescribed courses. Does the fact that one has completed the requirements for graduation make him an "educated man"? We don't know. But we do know that those who perform well in the system—the four-year academic program—and receive high grades usually are excellent prospects as graduate students and, later, as college professors. We also know that many who do not go on to graduate school have apparently benefited from meeting the graduation requirements, but we really don't know how or how much.

The output model that fulfills the output objectives of the college described by these graduation requirements is the "incipient scholar." He is introduced to and instructed in the culture of academe. How could it be otherwise, since those who plan and carry out the process to achieve the model are academicians? If you would produce the scholar, have him do what the scholar does.

The Teaching Model: A Bureaucracy

To produce the incipient scholar, the college typically organizes its teaching function bureaucratically (see discussion in chapter 3, p. 64), that is:

(1) Organizational tasks are distributed among various positions as official duties, to provide a clear-cut division of labor and make possible a high degree of specialization and expertness on the part of an incumbent;

(2) The positions or offices are organized into an hierarchical authority structure, with scope of authority of superiors over subordinates clearly circumscribed by rules protecting the prerogatives of the officeholder as he fulfills the duties of his office;

(3) A formally established system of rules and regulations governs official decisions and actions, within which officials are expected to assume an impersonal and objective relationship with their clients.[5]

The college breaks down its teaching function into relatively routine specialized tasks performed by many different experts. There is a clear-cut division of labor, with professors assigned to teach specific courses in various disciplines, academic deans to administer academic requirements, personnel deans to minister to the non-academic needs of the student, and deans of admission to ensure the proper student input into the system.

With so many different experts involved in the teaching function, the need for continuity is critical. A formally established system of rules and regulations is required to ensure equal and objective treatment of clients (students) and reasonable standardization of the ultimate product, the graduate. The rules and regulations are rational and impersonal—for example, course requirements, minimum grade average, minimum and maximum course load per semester or quarter. They are enforced by the bureaucratic hierarchy rationally, impersonally, and objectively: by the professor in the classroom as he meets his class at the prescribed hour and gives his examination, by the department head as he administers the department's instructional program, by the dean as he administers the instructional program.

But anyone who has been on a college campus for long knows that a professor is more than the bottom man in the bureaucratic hierarchy, carrying out orders of an administrative superior. He enjoys considerable autonomy in deciding what he will teach and how he will teach it. His right to do so is protected by additional rules and regulations—not always written—which circumscribe the authority which may be exercised over him by his bureaucratic superiors. He has been employed because of his expertness—mastery of some aspect of human knowledge—and it is not rational (and bureaucracies *are* rational) to so prescribe his actions that he cannot utilize his expertise.

A Framework for Expertise

Rules and regulations designed on the one hand to promote continuity and on the other hand to protect the right of the expert to make decisions pose the basic dilemma for bureaucratic organizations.[6] To reconcile this dilemma, colleges have generally ensured continuity by requiring the professors to exercise their expertness in a framework of regularly scheduled courses, covering a specialized category of human knowledge, offered to a prescribed group of students—freshmen, sophomores, juniors—who are examined on their mastery of that knowledge and graded according to their mastery. The colleges promote the exercise of expert autonomy within this framework by permitting the professor to decide what he will teach. (Within certain limits: for example, the professor of political science is not long permitted to teach physics in a course titled "American Political Parties," nor is the professor in a department permitted to deviate so far from the agreed-upon course content that it has no relevance to other courses in the department.) Further, the professor may decide how he will teach and grade students, provided that he meets his classes regularly and grades at regular intervals using the agreed-upon symbols.

This brief description of the bureaucratic organization of the college has not considered the role played by the faculty in establishing the rules and regulations of the college's teaching function. Faculty is empowered to make rules and regulations governing academic requirements of the college. However, in actual practice the faculty confines its rule-making to modifying course requirements or course content within the academic framework, for the faculty is typically committed to the model of the incipient scholar and to current practices to produce him. By virtue of their training, their commitment, and their primary work assignments, faculty members owe primary allegiance to one discipline, one aspect of human knowledge, and not to the totality of scholarship or to the total education of an individual. Thus, though the faculty has real power in deciding what, how, and whom to teach, its exercise of that power is well prescribed, and is therefore highly predictable.

The Admissions Role: Student Input

The two models thus far presented have real significance for the admissions officer, for they are sufficiently generalizable to be applied to most if not all liberal arts colleges. The admissions officer is placed in the college hierarchy with a defined set of functions that are designed to recruit and select students who fit a prototype of the potential scholar and who can accommodate themselves to the bureaucratic structure design to produce this scholar. Colleges differ in student input and output prototypes in degree, not in kind. One may select only students from the top 10 percent of the high school population while another may select from the top half: the former may expect 70 percent of its graduates to attend graduate school while the latter may have no more than 10 percent go on for graduate study. But each college will expect its admissions officers to possess the expertise to recruit and select students who can meet its minimum standards.

The priority of function for the admissions officer varies from college to college. For example, he may be primarily concerned with recruitment at one, but primarily with selection at another; with admitting a class all capable of at least a C+ average at one, and with selecting the best from a mediocre-to-poor applicant pool at another. But in all his cases his office is responsible for student inputs: his is the office that requires its incumbent to decide which students to admit, based on his knowledge of applicant availability and characteristics of successful students at his college. Of course, at most colleges the admissions officer cannot unilaterally decide questions of admissions. But it is the nature of bureaucracies to promote expertness—in fact, to require it. The admissions officer, because he is full time and because typically he is trained to understand and to deal with the problems inherent in recruiting and selecting students, does in fact become the expert in these activities. His expertness, plus the legal authority of his bureaucratic office, means that his decisions determine the *real* admissions practices of the college—faculty and bureaucratic superiors notwithstanding. Faculty and bureaucratic superiors do have the right of review of the admissions officer's actions, but this is likely to be exercised only if the decisions made by the admissions officer deviate markedly from generally accepted admissions policy and result in a marked change in the composition of the incoming class: if, for example, too few students matriculate to fill available beds in the dormitories, or if a larger percentage of students fail than past experience indicates should have failed, or if a smaller percentage of students fit the scholar prototype of the college than fitted it in past years.

Though similarities of output model and teaching model exist among colleges, critical differences exist among colleges in their achievement of their output model and in their bureaucratic structure to achieve it. Such differences are crucial to the admissions officer, since the many prescriptions for his actions in the literature are relevant only to the degree that his college is similar to the college for which they were prescribed. Though the admissions office may know that the teaching function of colleges is to produce the incipient scholar, and that they are organized bureaucratically to this end, he must still identify the idiosyncratic type of scholar his college is producing and the idiosyncratic processes used to produce that scholar.

Key Factor: The College's Real Aims

A key to identifying such idiosyncrasies is a knowledge of the *real* purposes of a college. Unfortunately for the admissions officer, these purposes are never stated. What the college typically states as its purposes, usually found in its bulletin, are such idealized output objectives as "to produce the educated man," "to furnish man's knowledge through research," "to serve the community or the nation by promoting free inquiry."

The true purposes of colleges are to satisfy one of four needs: survival, commergence, differentiation, and self-actualization. (See chapter 1.)

The four needs are ranked hierarchically. Once the survival need is satisfied the need for commergence becomes dominant; once the commergence need is satisfied the need for differentiation takes priority; and finally, when the differentiation need is fulfilled, the self-actualization need becomes paramount.

When the overriding need of a college is to survive, admission of students is a financial necessity. The college must recruit enough students to meet the payroll; never mind whether they meet the scholar prototype of the faculty. "Good" students are sought, but the basic question for the admissions officer is quantity, not quality.

Admission of students when the survival need is dominant has the attention of the top administrative officials, because recruitment of enough students is essential to the continued existence of the college. Probably the president and certainly the business manager of the college will be closely involved in recruitment and selection of students. The faculty's involvement may well be minimal—not for any lack of interest on their part, but because they recognize that quality of students is a moot point until the college is assured of enough students to survive.

After survival: the need to belong. Once a college is assured of enough students to survive, it alters its admissions practices to meet the need for commergence—the need "to belong," to be accepted as one of the colleges that "belong." The primary purpose now is to achieve the status of and be accepted by those colleges that maintain "standards" to ensure that their students meet the requisites of potential scholars. No longer is the college content merely to enroll enough students. It now needs to be certain that a reasonable number of them will graduate as incipient scholars.

It is time for the college to join the College Board, to publish its freshman class profile, to collect data on its students so that grade-point averages for incoming students may be accurately predicted. The time when students were in short supply is still fresh in the memory of some officials of the college and possibly of some of the faculty, but selectivity, within reason, is the mode. Of the students who apply, the "best" are to be taken. Though faculty and administration recognize that some students must be admitted who do not much resemble potential scholars, every effort is made to admit all who show some such ressemblance.

The next step, from commergence to differentiation, is a big jump: from the need to belong, to be one of a group of colleges that actually select their students, to the need of being different while belonging. Differentiation is fulfilled only when the college is first among equals, when the college can be more selective than other colleges in the "selective admissions club." Now the college takes real pride as its average College Board scores rise steadily, as the high school rank of its admitted students places most of them in the top quarter and then in the top tenth of their graduation classes. This desire to be different is a desire to be different in degree, not in kind. The college accepts with little question the potential scholar as its admissions prototype and the incipient scholar as its graduate prototype. Its major concern is to admit only those who truly match its admissions prototype: all likely candidates for rigorous graduate study.

The faculty is now surely involved in the admissions process, in establishing admissions policy and possibly even in helping the admissions officer to administer it. The administration, no longer seeing students as a means to survival or a means to belonging, is reasonably secure and accurate in its statement that admissions is the domain of the faculty.

Still no contentment. One might think that a college, once it met the differentiation need, would rest on its laurels and bask in the envy of those colleges still striving to move from survival to commergence, or from commergence to differentiation. But some colleges, now first among equals, are not content merely to be the best of a group where excellence is measured by such criteria as College Board scores and rank in high school class of students admitted, or the percentage of graduates entering graduate school. For these colleges, the discontents, the need for self-actualization assumes dominance, and they become pacesetters in creating new patterns of teaching, of curriculum, of admissions. They may well stop publishing a freshman class profile, admit on an experimental basis groups of students who do not meet traditional admissions standards, or emphasize such "nonacademic" criteria in selecting students as low socioeconomic background, positions of leadership in high school, or a history of after-school employment. This is not to say that such colleges will not consider traditional academic criteria in admissions, for they will. But as they attempt to satisfy the self-actualization need they will also admit students who are poor risks when judged by academic criteria.

Obviously such a departure in admissions criteria has significant implications for the curriculum and instruction of the college. Were curriculum and instruction not to reflect the change in admissions standards, it would be disastrous for many of the admitted students who deviated markedly from old and validated standards. A college meeting the self-actualization need does alter its instructional program. Special programs are introduced for those students who cannot initially meet the rigors of the regular academic program. (These programs are not simply screening devices, as they may be when established at some colleges forced to take unqualified students.) These special programs may deemphasize courses and grades and may be structured along the lines of much graduate education—particularly in medical schools and some Ph.D. programs—to emphasize the development of the individual student in a flexible and highly personal learning environment. Close contact among students and between the faculty and students becomes the rule. The faculty assume that the student can and will succeed; evaluation becomes highly personal and subjective; and most students do, in fact, succeed. The college has not forsaken the output model of the incipient scholar nor the bureaucratic organization designed to produce him. It has, however, committed itself to the proposition that (1) there may be other output models that can be accommodated by a more flexible approach to instruction and (2) there are different and possibly more effective means of producing the incipient scholar than the accepted pattern of semester courses, examinations, and grades.

Why labels don't work. This discussion of the hierarchy of needs and the consequent purpose priorities of colleges could leave the impression that colleges can simply be labeled "survival" or "commergent," and that the label thereby explains what kind of admissions practices they employ. Such an impression would indeed be naive, for even the college fighting for survival has its eye on the day when it can focus on satisfying the commergence need. It may, though on a modest scale, be experimenting after the fashion of the college at the stage of self-actualization. What we hope this discussion of college needs and purposes has done is demonstrate that the needs of the college dictate the priority of purposes and functions of the college. When survival is the dominant need, all purposes and functions of admissions practices will be measured in terms of their contribution to the survival to the college. But college needs and purposes are constantly changing; even while the college is focusing on survival it is making some effort to prepare to meet the needs of commergence.

Must the college move up the needs hierarchy in lock-step fashion? No one can say for sure, but it is doubtful that a college can jump from survival to differentiation, for, after all, a college must be accepted, must belong to the ingroup, before it can be recognized as the "best" member of that group. Society does not usually accept an organization that deviates from the norm until it demonstrates that it can meet the demands of the norm. It is not usually the nature of the high school graduate, if he has a choice in the college he will attend, to select one that deviates markedly from the scholar output model and the bureaucratic model unless that college has already demonstrated that it can produce the scholar utilizing the traditional mode.

Where the Admissions Officer Fits

As a bureaucratic officer in the college hierarchy, the admissions officer is charged with the recruitment and selection of students. Priorities for performing the varied functions necessary to the recruitment and selection of students are largely determined by the dominant purposes or needs of the college in which the admissions officer works. When the survival need is paramount, his primary function is to recruit students. Quality of students is not a major consideration; quantity is. He probably will report to an administrative officer charged with the business and financial affairs of the college, or at least work closely with that official. The admissions officer at Survival College may report directly to the president, since the recruitment of students is so critical to the continued operation of the college. This is true not only of private colleges but also of state colleges "on the rise" that depend on legislative largesse, which is based on enrollments, for expanding facilities and increasing faculty.

At Survival College, the admissions officer will be judged primarily on his ability to attract students to the college. Though he may be expected to know more than effective recruitment techniques—how to compute a regression equation and interpret test scores, how to interpret to the faculty certain high school curriculum trends, and how admission is conducted at other colleges—his basic job is to recruit and deliver on opening day the expected number of students.

At Commergent College the admissions officer is still concerned with recruiting students, but he is now also expected to select the best from those recruited. He must be competent in the use of various prediction instruments and in interpreting those instruments to the faculty and administration. He must be skilled in working with the faculty, for at this level it is surely involved in admissions and will want to know why more "good" students are not being admitted. The admissions officer may now report to an academic dean to ensure the maintenance of admissions standards and the upgrading of those standards.

The admissions officer at Commergent College is likely to occupy a most difficult position. He is expected to select capable students from an applicant pool that has a limited number of such students. Though some potential scholar prototypes will be admitted, the admissions officer will still need to admit some marginal students. He will be under pressure to tighten up on admissions standards and at the same time secure enough students to fill the freshman quota. His relations with high school counselors will reflect those pressures. Counselors have come to see Commergent College as a place for some of their marginal students, but now some of those marginal students are being denied admission. Also, the admissions officer, intent on improving the caliber of students applying, is asking the counselor embarrassing questions: "Why do none of your top students ever apply to our college?" "Why are many of the students we admit from your school in academic trouble at the end of their freshman year?"

At the college where the differentiation need is dominant, the admissions officer's problems have become problems of riches. He now can select his freshman class from an applicant pool all of whom, on paper at least, exhibit the qualities of successful students. He is now concerned with selecting those students who are the "best," for Differentiation College is known for its high standards of admissions. High school counselors will not encourage a student to apply whose College Board scores are much below 600, whose grade average is less than B, or whose rank in class is below the top quarter (and in some cases the top 10 percent). The admissions officer is still concerned with recruiting students, but the reputation of the college does much of this job for him. He is no longer worried about getting enough qualified applicants, those who are able to do a creditable (C average) academic job. But he is concerned with finding more applicants capable of doing a superior academic job.

Still, the admissions officer at Differentiation College faces his share of embarrassing questions. Alumni are asking: "Is the college interested only in the A student?" Some faculty are asking: "Why do some of these students who are supposed to be so good show so little imagination and intellectual curiosity?" Some faculty, some alumni, and some administrators are asking: "Why don't more of our students come from the lower-middle or upper-lower classes?" "Don't most of our students look, talk, and act too much alike, to the point that our campus isn't really a very exciting place?" "Isn't it time we did some experimentation with our admissions practices—admit, say, a few talented artists, musicians, and student leaders who may not have been good students in high school and may not have particularly high test scores?"

Most of these questions the admissions officer can answer directly, but he probably won't. Instead, he'll say, "We have chosen to become the best among colleges which have as their basic teaching objective the production of scholars. We have quite rationally organized our teaching to produce those scholars, and we have geared our admissions practices to select those students most able to succeed in our system. If we are taking mostly A students, it is because A students seem to succeed better than B or C students. If we are not getting the artist or the musician, it may be that our system does not appeal to him or that he does not present the high-quality admissions credentials we require. If our students seem much alike, it is because they *are* much alike: they have similar interests, family backgrounds, high school experiences, and occupational objectives." The admissions officer at Differentiation College is viewed as an expert at answering such questions. Though he errs now and then, for the most part the students admitted do quite well and the reputation of the college has never been better, in terms of graduates going on to graduate school and the academic records they make while attending.

At Self-Actualization College, the faculty, the administration, and the admissions officer have seriously questioned the incipient scholar output model and the bureaucratic teaching model as the only appropriate ones for the college's instructional function. Experimentation is the word of the day, the week, and the year. Students are admitted who don't fit the potential-scholar prototype, though the college has in its applicant pool many more students than it can admit who fit that prototype quite well. The admissions director is encouraged to experiment with new and different criteria for admissions and, what is more, to help the faculty develop new curriculums and methods of instruction appropriate for the students admitted under the new admissions criteria. The admissions officer, though still a recruiter and a selector of students, is a good deal more. He is looked to by faculty and administration as an analyst of human behavior, an expert on learning environments, a full-fledged partner in the instructional process. He may well hold faculty rank—and not of the honorary variety—and be a recognized expert in learning and teaching.

To do more than describe the functions of the admissions officer, which is a limited service at best, one must assess the dominant needs or purposes of the college in which he works. To tell the admissions officer to stay at home and identify more with his faculty when students of any kind are needed for the college to survive is foolish; to tell the admissions officer that he should be a specialist in "learning environments" and devote most of his time to helping the faculty develop new curriculums when his college is striving to be accepted as a selective college is naive; to tell the admissions officer that he should concentrate on developing "nonacademic" criteria for admission when his college is proving that it is among the best colleges employing only an academic model is unrealistic; to tell the admissions officer that he should be consistent in employing "academic" criteria for admission when his college is charting a new course in education by employing not only an academic model is irrelevant.

All of this is not to say that the admissions officer should not become a more active force in the planning of the college curriculum; that he should not become an expert on the programs of secondary schools; that he should not be a first-rate statistician (and what is more, a sophisticate in research). These are worthy goals, and some admissions officer somewhere is probably all of them. But to be realistic one must recognize that the college environment largely predetermines what the admissions officer will give his first attention to. If he goes beyond the priority demands of his college—prescribed by the dominant need of the college—he does so on his own time and at his own risk. He must also recognize, however, that priorities change. It is in his best interests to anticipate changes rather than have them pointed out to him by a bureaucratic superior, or—even worse—by a committee of the faculty.

The University as an Instructional Bureaucracy

It is not our intent to show that colleges are totally bureaucratic organizations, for in fact they are not. Certainly their research functions are carried on in an organizational framework more professional than bureaucratic and their governance is often collegial rather than bureaucratic.[7] But their instructional function is highly bureaucratized.

The college subdivides its instructional function—the means to educate its students—into many discrete parts. One department is responsible for instruction in English, another for instruction in history, another for instruction in mathematics, and so on. Professors are chosen for their competence as specialists in a discipline such as English, history or mathematics, not for their competence as specialists in learning, in instruction, or in the overall process of education. Personnel deans minister to the nonacademic needs of the student and academic deans guide him into appropriate academic courses. This subdivision of labor encourages, even demands, increasing specialization and expertness by professors and deans in only one segment of instruction; the assumption is, apparently, that such specialization and expertness focusing on the parts of a student's education will strengthen the whole of his education.

The validation of such an assumption cannot be left to chance. Consequently, general rules and regulations exist to require each student to take a prescribed number of hours in specific disciplines and to maintain a minimum grade point average. Further, each academic department is required to offer courses meeting for a prescribed number of hours, to examine and grade students on the content of those courses. Such general rules and regulations also prescribe that each client (student) be treated objectively and impersonally as he meets the academic requirements of the college (though rules can be waived, they are not to be waived often).

College instruction, which involves so many experts and is governed by extensive rules and regulations, is controlled hierarchically to unite its discrete parts into a manageable whole, to coordinate the experts' efforts, to interpret and to administer the academic rules and regulations. Deans, assistant deans, department heads, and professors make up this hierarchy, deans at the top and professors at the bottom. (Again, let us emphasize that this bureaucratic and hierarchical arrangement applies to the instructional function of the college, not necessarily to its research function or indeed to its overall governance.) The faculty is empowered to overrule the hierarchy, to change the rules and regulations, but it very seldom does, for by virtue of their training, their disciplinary commitment, and their instructional assignments, faculty members owe primary allegiance to one discipline, one element of human knowledge. Their concern is with a part and not the whole of a student's education. Thus, once agreement is reached on courses, grade point averages, and total hours of instruction, they generally leave to selected bureaucratic officials the task of managing instruction.

Bureaucratic organization of college instruction is a response to a very real dilemma faced by colleges. Colleges, like all organizations, must achieve efficiency, order, and predictability of operation. On the other hand, education as a process is not necessarily efficient, orderly, or predictable. One college president succinctly pointed up this dilemma when he said: "We would love to teach education if we could find anyone who knew anything about it."[8]

Since the education of a student is so difficult to measure and since instruction as a means to educate the student is so complex a process, how can one justify organizing instruction bureaucratically? Bureaucracy seems best suited to organizations when ends are discrete and measurable, when means are clear and agreed on, and when causal relationships between means and ends are readily demonstrable.[9]

Insight into how colleges justify bureaucratizing instruction is gained by an analysis of the technology of instruction extant in most colleges. All organizations employ a technology: "a technique or complex of techniques used to alter materials (human or nonhuman—mental or physical) in an anticipated manner."[10] A technology requires a knowledge of cause and effect, a system of feedback to measure effect, replication of acts and results, and the ability to predict success. The technology employed largely prescribes the kind of organization in which it can be carried on.[11] The instructional technology of the college is based on a "closed system" concept of education: an education is what the college's instruction provides; students who do well in the system are then by definition educated.[12] Studies of the relation between college success (success in the college "system") and success after college (success in other "systems") indicate that success in college seems to be highly correlated with continued success in college and/or graduate school but is at best "moderately" correlated with adult success, no matter how defined.[13]

College instructional technology is designed to produce "incipient scholars," students who do well in college and later in graduate school. When the end of college instruction is the production of incipient scholars rather than education in a broader context, present instruction in colleges does meet the requisites of a technology. There is an a priori knowledge of cause—the college's instruction—and effect—production of incipient scholars, since only those who attend and do well in college become scholars. There is a system of feedback to measure the effect of instruction, since student grades from one year to the next show a high relationship and grades in undergraduate school do correlate highly with grades in graduate school. The acts of instruction and their results can be and are replicated from year to year. Finally of real signficance to the admissions officer, the effect on students (of the college's instructional technology) can be reasonably well predicted. Students who have done well in school and present high aptitude and achievement test scores will usually do better in college than those who have done poorly in high school and/or present low aptitude and achievement test scores.

The technology employed largely prescribes the organization that accommodates it: When cause and effect are known, decisions can be made by using "computational strategies," "rational calculation"; and bureaucracy is a form of organization ideally suited for efficient and effective use of "computational strategies" and "rational calculations."[14]

What position does the admissions officer occupy in this bureaucratic organization for instruction? He is the expert bureaucrat assigned to standardize student "input" into the college system, the keeper-at-the-gate to student applications. His task is to select those students who are most likely to succeed in college, who will respond most positively to the kind of instruction the college provides. He is aided by faculty committees dedicated to this same end, by high school counselors whose job it is to "guide" students toward the "right" college, by increasingly comprehensive instruments for measuring students' scholastic achievement, and by sophisticated statistical methods for predicting college scholastic achievement.

To perform better his task as bureaucrat for standardizing student input, the admissions officer strives to admit only applicants who will be good students, maintaining at least a C average but hopefully better than C. This means that he seeks to improve the reliability and validity of the criteria that predict academic performance in college.

To improve the reliability and validity of his predictions, the admissions officer might well consider the bureaucratic organization of instruction, which has thus far received little notice by those attempting to predict college success. What are some possible characteristics of students that are likely to predict their positive response to bureaucratized instruction (characteristics other than those revealed by tests, which indicate a certain level of literacy and scholastic achievement, and grades and rank in class, which indicate literacy and scholastic achievement and also the extent to which a student has accommodated himself to bureaucratized instruction in high school)? We offer three significant characteristics:

(1) The student's ability to accept as a meaningful goal the completion of a course, whether or not the course is personally interesting or stimulating and whether or not it seems to have any relevance to any other interests and goals the student might have;

(2) His ability to separate feeling from intellect, and personal relationships from academic work;

(3) His ability to seek and perhaps to demand "closure," to think convergently, to categorize in the face of all manner of uniqueness so that he can accept a given college course as a self-contained unit, not necessarily relevent to anything preceding or following it.

But suppose the college admissions officer is not content to remain the bureaucrat for student input standardization. Suppose he is not even willing to accept the present bureaucratic pattern of instruction as the only pattern for most colleges or the best pattern for many students. Can he do anything—other than resign?

What may appear to be the most obvious thing to do—to alter the exisiting bureaucratic pattern of instruction—is impractical, unrealistic, and certain to fail. First of all, the present pattern of instruction is self-validating at many colleges. They have on the average seven applicants for every student admitted; one doesn't quarrel with that kind of success. Secondly, the present bureaucratic organization of instruction seems to be most successful at those colleges that are members of the educational elite and have the most prestigious facilities, the highest admissions standards, and the highest percentage of students going on to graduate school. The admissions director who suggests departing from the mode of instruction such "elites" employ risks the charge that strikes fear in the hearts of all admissions men, veteran and fledgling alike: "*You have lowered standards.*" Finally, there is little to be gained by changing the bureaucratic organization of instruction until the present technology of instruction is modified through a broadened definition of a college education and the means to attain it.

> The plea is not to lower standards but to individualize them more; to encourage and stimulate personal development in whatever dimensions it is best expressed. To be concrete, it means we would be willing to "forgive" a student his inability (or unwillingness) to master a foreign language if he manifested alternative signs of personal development (e.g., composed publishable music, developed his potential for leadership).[15]

If the admissions officer believes that his college can and should help students develop as artists, or teachers, or musicians, or social workers, and not just incidentally and accidentally outside the instructional organization designed to produce the incipient scholar, he can show the way toward experimentation designed to identify desirable and appropriate educational ends and the means to achieve them. If the admissions officer believes that his college should and can contribute measurably to the development of students' leadership ability, or social commitment or creativity, then it behooves him to contribute substantively toward building new technologies of instruction, not necessarily to replace but rather to complement present instructional technology.

We are proposing that colleges establish additional instructional technologies, in a framework of controlled experimentation. Surely no self-respecting faculty is unwilling to engage in research and experimentation, particularly in what many believe is the business of the college: education. Programs could be established for a select group of students, unfettered by existing course requirements, course sequences, semester grades, and possibly even courses themselves now constituted. Such programs would consider the strengths and weaknesses of students admitted, the students' interests and his tentative educational objectives, and the objectives of the college—how the college program is to change the student.

Colleges that remain fully committed to the incipient scholar as the objective of their instruction could experiment with more flexible and imaginative ways to produce him. Several colleges, e.g., Duke and Harvard, have programs for culturally and educationally deprived students that deviate from their regular course programs and emphasize special tutorials, flexible course requirements, and moderate GPA standards, at least for the freshman year.

Other, more radical colleges could experiment with instructional technologies and organizations other than those appropriate for producing the incipient scholar. The incipient scholar model is not the only appropriate one for educating students to enter such fields as the performing arts, nursing, elementary school teaching, social work, accounting, and sales.

And the admissions officer? In some colleges he will be concerned solely with guarding the gate, making certain that the instructional bureaucracy is not unduly disturbed by an input of students who don't fit. In other colleges he will be charged with helping to select as freshmen small groups of students who don't "fit" but who can, with the help of special academic dispensations, tutors, and remedial courses, be made to fit by the second or third year in residence. (Many colleges have provided such programs, for some time, for athletes, so it should not be too radical a step to provide such programs for artists, youngsters from the black ghetto, campus leaders, or even sons of alumni.) Finally, in some colleges, a minority at first to be sure, the admissions officer will play a major role in promoting "important new departures in the teaching and learning process at the undergraduate level. . . . What is learned will have increased relevance to the process of lifelong education, to cultivating the habit of learning and the appetite for it. For the first time, we shall educate for coping with a changing environment."[16] Such colleges are emerging in many of our larger cities. These urban colleges and universities view education as a continuing, lifelong process, and see no basic conflict between training and education, between work and study, between educational standards and the multiplicity of human talent.

The admissions officer whose sole function is that of bureaucrat for student input standardization can soon be replaced—and probably should be—by the computer. There will always be a need for personable, alert, and dedicated young men to represent colleges at college nights, to soothe disappointed parents and disillusioned students rejected by the college of their choice. But, in the main, decisions about admissions will be made by a computer programmed with the appropriate regression equation and data furnished by high schools and testing agencies.

The admissions officer who is a bit more than bureaucrat for student input standardization—let us call him bureaucrat for standardization, modified—who is trying to select students that do not fit initially the instructional bureaucracy designed to produce incipient scholars, will still play a significant role in admissions. He will help develop new criteria for predicting academic success; our previous suggestions about student attributes that will indicate which students can readily accommodate themselves to bureaucratized instruction merit this admissions officer's consideration. Not only will he be expected to broaden the base of admissions, to include more students who don't fit, but he will also devote no little time to helping the faculty develop the kinds of programs for such students to bring them up to the "standard" demanded by the instructional bureaucracy, hopefully by their sophomore year, certainly by their junior year.

The college committed to producing more than the incipient scholar requires a new kind of admissions officer, who can take the lead in developing means to measure the education potential of entering students; work with faculty in developing instructional technologies designed to educate the different kinds of students admitted; and assist in developing the means for measuring the effect of the college's instruction on the student.

We need be little concerned with the training of the bureaucrat for student input standardization; he will soon be extinct. Present selection and training for the bureaucrat for student input standardization, modified, must be improved if he is to devise new criteria for student selection and assist in developing one- or two-year orientation programs designed to prepare students for the rigors of the instructional bureaucracy.

There are at present no systematic methods of selecting, educating, or training the new admissions officers, who must not only know present admissions practices but also be sophisticated in the use and development of instruments for evaluating student potential. They must be expert in instructional technologies, their organization and evaluation. Some are now learning on the job, as admissions officers at rapidly expanding, comprehensive colleges–most of them publicly supported. It would be sad indeed if their selection and training were left to chance. They would learn through trial and error that the roles of bureaucrat for student input standardization and bureaucrat for student input standardization, modified, are totally inappropriate for them, but they would learn at the expense of their colleges and their students. The cost of their learning is more than society should or needs to bear.

Notes for Chapter 4

1. Nevitt Sanford, ed., *The American College* (New York: John Wiley & Sons, 1962), p. 10.
2. Bernard S. Adams, "A new pattern for admissions officers," *College Board Review* no. 49 (winter 1963).
3. Gordon A. Sabine, "Is there static in the educational channel?" *College Board Review* no. 51 (fall 1963).
4. These models are adapted from a discussion of the characteristics of colleges by John J. Corson, *Governance of Colleges and Universities* (New York: McGraw-Hill Book Co., 1960), pp. 8-11.
5. Amitai Etzioni, *Modern Organizations* (Englewood Cliffs, N.J.: Prentice-Hall, 1964), pp. 50-57. (Adapted from Etzioni's discussion of Weber's definition of bureaucracy.)
6. For a full discussion of this organizational dilemma, see Peter M. Blau and W. Richard Scott, *Formal Organizations* (San Francisco: Chandler Publishing Co., 1962), pp. 242-250.
7. For discussion of professional versus bureaucratic authority, see Etzioni, *Modern Organizations*, pp. 75-79.
8. *College Board Review*, no. 61 (fall 1966): 32.
9. Blau and Scott, *Formal Organizations*, pp. 206-210 .
10. Charles Perrow, "Hospitals: Technology, Structure, and Goals," in *Handbook of Organizations*, ed. James March (Chicago: Rand McNally, 1965), p. 915.
11. Ibid., pp. 915-916.
12. B. Alden Thresher, *College Admissions and the Public Interest* (New York: College Entrance Examination Board, 1966), pp. 47-54.
13. Donald P. Hoyt, "The Relationship between College Grades and Adult Achievement, A Review of the Literature" (a pamphlet), *ACT Research Reports*,

no. 7 (Iowa City: American College Testing Program, 1965).

14. Blau and Scott, *Formal Organizations,* pp. 41-42.

15. Hoyt, "The Relationship between College Grades and Adult Achievement," p. 49.

16. Thresher, *College Admissions and the Public Interest,* p. 85.

Part 2

How to Survive in and Change Educational Organizations: Operational Guides to Decision-Making

Part 1 focused on the milieu or setting in which the decision-maker in educational organizations operates. The fact that we spent so much time in building a framework for understanding educational organizations indicates our belief that decisions are not made in a vacuum; effective decision-making depends on an understanding of the setting in which decision-making takes place. In discussing educational organizations, we have already identified many of the variables that decision-makers must take into account, e.g., individual and group needs and desires, available resources, rewards and sanctions, group norms, and informal influence patterns.

It is precisely the way in which the decision-maker relates to and manipulates these variables that determines his effectiveness in educational organizations. This is the subject of Part 2, "How to Survive In and Change Educational Organizations."

To give some structure or organization to different ways in which organizational variables can be manipulated, and to stimulate discussion and debate, in chapters 5, 6, 7, and 8, we have identified a series of operational guides to decision-making that we think take into account the various dimensions of the decision-making process. These guides have philosophical, psychological, and technical overtones. They are philosophical in that they reflect what we as authors think should be the case in educational decision-making, they are psychological in that they influence how the decision-maker feels about himself and others, and they are technical in that they explain to some extent how to achieve one's goals and objectives efficiently.

Part 2 is designed to enable you as an educational decision-maker to place yourself in various situations that require you to make decisions concerning instruction directly, or decisions about variables within the educational organizations having a close relationship to instruction. Part 2 contains several operational guides to decision-making. Those guides have been developed out of experience in dealing with organizational dilemmas in schools and colleges and through study of organizational and instructional theory. They do not offer absolute answers in any decision-making situation, but if they help you understand the variables you are dealing with a bit better, and make your decisions more effective, they have served their purpose. You are of course encouraged to formulate your own operational guides.

There are references to educational organizations as government agencies or government organizations. Obviously not all schools and colleges are governmentally controlled, but the governance of educational organizations, public or private, appears to be quite similar, and statements about governance functions seem as appropriate for private schools and colleges as for public schools and colleges.

In our discussion of instructional functions, the influence of the bureaucratic model on them is referred to frequently. This model is discussed in detail in chapters 3 and 4, and is compared with what we deem a more appropriate model for instruction, the professional model.

Every decision-maker has his own value hierarchy, whether he is aware of it or not. One of our aims in this book is to aid the teacher in understanding what he values and how much he values what he says and thinks he values. In other words, the decision-maker should know himself. A second dimension of decision-making is the importance of knowing your educational organization. The decision-maker who knows himself can better relate to the values supported by the educational organization in which he operates. A third dimension deals with the subject of knowing how to change what you think needs changing in your organization as well as yourself. Strategies for changing the organization are, however, more effective when the decision-maker knows himself and the organization in which he is working. Our view of the relationship between the three dimensions of decision-making is illustrated in the following figure.

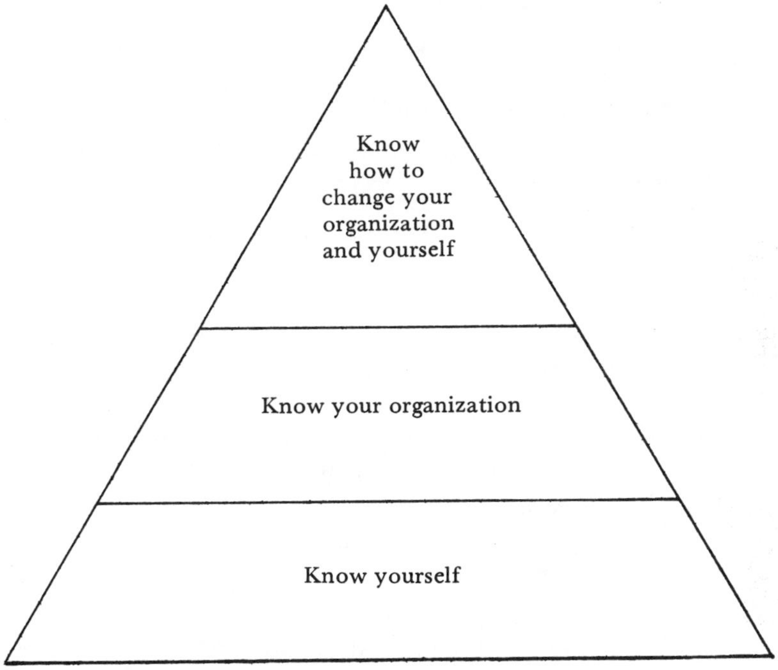

Three Dimensions of Decision-Making

The decision-maker who begins at the "how to change it" level without benefit of knowledge of himself or the school as an organization is inconsistent, and this will be indicated in his decision-making pattern. His disorientation will be apparent. He may appear to be charismatic and dynamic but the zigs and zags in his decision-making pattern will show that he is seriously lacking in logically consistent underpinnings. The decision-maker who begins at the "know your organization" level without accurate knowledge of himself will simply be a midwife for the ideas of others.

Each operational guide in the following chapters has three dimensions: (1) know yourself, (2) know your organization, and (3) know how to change the organization and yourself.

Before proceeding further, let us discuss a value hierarchy that will give the reader an opportunity to examine how intensely he supports any given value. A basic assumption on which the value hierarchy is built is that values have little meaning unless they are related to consequences. If, for example, a person tells us he believes in freedom, this reveals very little unless we know how far he will commit himself in his actions in behalf of freedom. Our hierarchy consists of six levels of intensity or depth of commitment in descending order:

If I cannot continue to do a certain thing or if I am required to do a certain thing,

(1) I will sacrifice my life and/or the lives of my family and/or those I dearly love;

(2) I will give up the respect of those whom I love and I'll forego my status and professional achievement;

(3) I will forego economic security and my career;

(4) I will have serious conflicts between what I think should be done and my reluctance to do it. I may have to alter my work style and give up those techniques which had previously been successful and beneficial and learn new ones;

(5) I will have to alter some habits with which I'm quite comfortable, thus making my job somewhat more difficult. I will feel uncomfortable from time to time as I'll do things that don't seem to be the best way to do them based on my past experience and present assumptions.

(6) It doesn't make any difference as past experience indicates. My choice, therefore, is between tweedledee and tweedledum.

It should be obvious to the decision-maker that different people's values and beliefs are placed in priority for any given situation, and it is through looking at the pattern of one's decisions that we can understand the decision-making style of the individual. Jane's friend Susan asks Jane what she thinks of her new hair style. Although Jane doesn't especially like the new hair style, she knows that Susan does and so she says she likes it even though she doesn't. She reasoned that a "little lie" wouldn't cost her anything and would in fact probably reap benefits in terms of Susan's positive attitude toward her. A low priority item for Jane was a high priority item for Susan and a trade-off was made: a "little lie" for approbation. If Jane makes similar trade-offs on a variety of issues to receive the approval of others, it would be clear that this was part of her decision-making style; if not, it would appear that there are other values that she holds higher and this is reflected in her decision-making style. The upshot is that the decision-maker should recognize that he or she and others have different levels of commitment to any value that place such decisions at different levels of our value hierarchy.

A second generalization about the hierarchy of values and decision-making is that it is wise to keep from escalating on the value hierarchy whenever possible. For example, the issue of long hair in public schools should be at level 6 or at the most 5. The higher the issue is on the hierarchy, the greater the chance that students and faculty will face an impasse. This creates the conditions for further conflict on what should be issues of the tweedledee and tweedledum nature.

A related generalization is that the decision-maker should de-escalate whenever possible. To do so creates conditions for a more rational and normal situation whereby different members of the school as a sociopolitical system can go about their work.

In our discussion of the operational guides for decision-making in the following chapters we will refer to the value hierarchy again. It is our intention in exploring the various operational guides to place the reader in the position of decision-maker whenever possible. As such it is important to realize that all situations in which human interaction takes place can be understood in terms of action-reaction. Another way to state this is to say that there is from moment to moment an actor and a reactor. The main advantage in the acting rather than reacting role is that the actor usually controls more variables in the situation than those who must react to his offensive. Football provides us with an excellent analogy. The team on offense selects the kind of play to be run, the timing, the personnel to be used, and thereby has a great advantage over the team on defense. Rules limiting what the offense can do are necessary to prevent the team on offense from scoring every time it gets the ball. For example, only one backfield player can be in motion at a time, no movement by offensive linemen can be made until the ball is snapped, and there are a limited number of eligible pass receivers. To play the game many more restrictions must be placed on the team on offense than on the team on defense.

There is disagreement among authorities on decision-making as to how rationality is, can, and should be used in decision-making. Some argue that one makes a decision based on a value or personal preference and then proceeds to rationalize the decision; others contend that there are rational processes involved in all stages of good decision-making. Our view is that regardless of one's position about this issue, rationality plays an important role. That is, it must be used in all cases to explain or justify a decision previously made and it certainly should be a major factor in making all decisions. The greater the extent to which the decision-maker is the actor rather than the reactor, the greater his chance for rational input because he exercises greater control over the time, the place, and the situation. This also increases his responsibility to be rational, which in turn increases his responsibility for his actions.

Key Variables in Decision-Making

There are certain key variables involved in effective decision-making, each of which must be taken into account in the operational guides.

The first variable is knowing what you want to achieve. We sometimes refer to this as objectives, goals, or desired outcomes. To fail to recognize the importance of this variable is to let outside forces dictate how one will behave.

A second variable is resources. The decision-maker must recognize what resources are presently available, what resources will *probably* be available in the future, and what resources will *possibly* be available. This knowledge will help him make wise decisions as to how to maximize a finite number of resources given an infinite number of wants.

The decision-maker also needs to know those obstacles that presently exist, those obstacles that will probably exist in the future, and those obstacles that may possibly exist at some time in the future.

A fourth variable that the decision-maker needs to consider is the alternative courses of action available to reach one's objectives. As there is no "right" answer in facing a dilemma, this is one of the most critical tasks facing the decision-maker.

Timing is another critical variable. What resources should the decision-maker use at different times during the decision-making process? The wise decision-maker will have a sensitive eye for what should occur at what time.

A sixth variable deals with the decision-maker's evaluation of what is happening at different stages of the decision-making process. How can he best acquire and analyze feedback?

Finally, the decision-maker must have machinery for altering and generating new objectives, and/or courses of action, and/or timing. The plan must be firm enough to instill confidence and flexible enough to find new and better directions.

The challenge to the decision-maker is sometimes minsinterpreted to mean that a person should immediately begin to change the entire organization. Polemicists often add to this view with messianic pleas: "If you're not for changing the organization you're against us!" "If you're not part of the solution you're part of the problem!" The very emotional fervor of many educational polemicists lends support to the view that there are some good guys and many bad guys.

Many polemicists' views as to change in educational organizations are naive, misleading, and dysfunctional. The most powerful person in an educational organization, whether he is a superintendent of schools or a university president, is not omnipotent and omniscient and cannot single-handedly change the entire organization. We urge you, the educational decision-maker, to try to change that part of the organization that affects you and is important to your value system. This is to say that you should "stick your toe in the water" and see how your decision-making affects a limited part of the organization. This experience will give you increased confidence so that you will then expand your influence into other areas of the school or university. "The democrat does not set out to abolish hell or bring heaven overnight; he is more interested in free lunches or increasing the income tax by 2 percent than in providing the final answer to the problem of poverty and suffering."[1]

We should like to offer a framework of questions that the decision-maker might well use to understand better the educational organization he is analyzing. The reader is encouraged to make any revisions he wishes in this framework, including the addition of questions he feels need to be asked.

Questions to Ask When Encountering a New Organization (for example, a School)

(1) Who decides what teachers will teach here? who gets promoted? salary increases?

(2) What's happened recently? What new curriculum proposals have been initiated? by whom? how?

(3) What problems have occurred recently in the organization? Who decided they were problems? What was done? by whom?

(4) If you want to get something done, who would you see and what would you tell him or her?

(5) What are some things you want to do that you're unable to do with the present organization? How do you know you can't? rule? regulation? someone told you? feeling that it's against tradition?

(6) Is this organization different from other organizations you know? How?

(7) If you could replace three people in the organization, who would you replace and why would you replace them?

Examining Other Decision-Makers' Assumptions

Name____________________________Section____________Date________

Now that you have identified your own basic assumptions about what is worthwhile and valuable, examine the following assumptions that decision-makers often hold to be true and discuss their implications for curriculum and instruction.

Assumptions	*Implications for Curriculum and Instruction*
(1) Work is good.	__________________________
(2) The harder you work the more you will be rewarded.	__________________________
(3) Work is a necessary evil. That is, you must do what	

you have to do in order to do other really important things in life. ______________________

(4) You will not be rewarded if you work harder than the job specifically requires. ______________________

(5) Cooperation is the greatest single good in society. ______________________

(6) Man should be judged on how much he helps others achieve rather than on how much he achieves, on how much he helps others to know rather than on how much he knows. ______________________

(7) The ability to compete and win is the greatest single good in society. ______________________

(8) Man should be judged according to his ability to compete and win. ______________________

Examining Your Basic Assumptions

Name______________________Section__________Date______

Please list your basic assumptions about what is worthwhile or valuable in life. After you have done this, state the antithesis or opposite for each assumption in the right-hand-column.

Assumptions	*Antitheses*
(1)	(1)
(2)	(2)
(3)	(3)
(4)	(4)
(5)	(5)

What are the implications of your assumptions for curriculum and instruction? For example, assuming that ________________________, curriculum and instruction should ____________________________.

Three Factors in Decision-Making

The decision-maker must constantly keep in mind three factors: (1) the quality of the decision, (2) the extent to which the decision is acceptable to those who must implement it or help implement it, and (3) the time available for both making the decision and for implementing it.

The quality of the decision is to be judged primarily by the decision-maker; but as the decision is implemented and its results become known, that quality will, of course, be judged by many others. By quality we mean the extent to which the decision (1) complements the goals the decision-maker has adopted and (2) provides objectives congruent with those goals.

When the quality of a decision is the paramount consideration, one may choose not to consult anyone else if he feels that he has sufficient data and expertise to make a high-quality decision on his own. Or he may seek help from others, but he does so primarily because he believes that their contribution will enhance the quality of the decision. For example, if one plans a lesson with the quality of the lesson uppermost in his mind, he may or may not seek information from others, depending on how competent he feels to make a high-quality decision with the information already available to him.

When acceptance is uppermost in the mind of the decision-maker, he consults with those whose acceptance of the decision is critical. He is not primarily concerned with the quality of their input, for he knows that if the decision is to be accepted those involved in carrying it out must play a major part in making it. He also knows that no matter what the quality of the decision is, if those who must implement it are not committed to it, the decision in fact is not likely to be effectively implemented.

The factor of time will affect the extent to which quality and acceptability can be considered. If time is the key variable—for example, if the classroom is on fire—one can give little consideration to either quality or acceptability—evacuation of the class as quickly as possible is the obvious thing to do. In this instance time is the primary consideration and the decision-maker can give little attention to either quality or the acceptability of this decision.

Of what practical value is consideration of these three variables to those who make decisions in educational organizations? First, the variable of time is the one that must be viewed most critically, for it is often allowed to dictate many decisions made in educational organizations. This seems to be another educational paradox, since educational organizations by virtue of the nature of their tasks should view their operations as having a long-term span. They are not emergency organizations, such as a police unit or a fire-fighting unit. They have much more time than their decision-making styles would lead one to believe they do. If time is not a critical variable, and usually it should not be in an educational situation, the quality and/or acceptability of the decision should assume paramount importance to the educational decision-maker.

Focusing on quality and acceptability, let us look at some practical steps the educational decision-maker might take in making and in implementing his decisions. For quality, we would look to philosophy, psychology, and concepts of organizations and administration: to philosophy for those values that we are attempting to implement, support, and maintain; to psychology for the concepts and principles of learning; and to organizations and administration for the feasibility and practicality of carrying out any instructional plan we might devise. The quality of the decision will then be largely related to how well we do what we want to do with the resources available. The quality of a decision is related to (1) what it is we say we want to do, (2) the resources available for us to do it, and (3) the extent to which we do the best possible job with those resources available.

The acceptability of the decision is attested to by the degree to which those who must participate in its implementation are committed to it and carry it out. The cooperation and commitment may come from the students who are being taught, from colleagues whose support is needed, or from the hierarchical superiors who must support the decision. No matter from what group acceptance comes, it is widely believed, at least in our culture, that acceptance is more likely to come from those who have had a part—or feel they have had a part—in making the decisions that affect them. Thus, when the decision-maker believes that acceptability is of paramount importance, he focuses much of his effort on consultation with others to gain their acceptance of the decision made.

The ideal decision-making situation is of course one in which the quality of the decision and the acceptability of the decision to those who are consulted are fully congruent. The group that is to carry out the decision also possesses the expertise to make a high-quality decision. In this situation, everyone is consulted, first because they have a major knowledge contribution to make to the decision, and secondly because through their participation they are more likely to accept the decision. However, the ideal decision situation does not occur frequently. In fact, many decision-makers believe that it never occurs.

In most decision-making situations, judgments must be made by the decision-maker as to *time*—how much time is available for making the decision before it may be made for him by others; *quality*—the extent to which the decision must be of high quality in terms of meeting the overall goals of the decision-maker; and *acceptability*—the degree to which those who participate in carrying out the decision need to be committed.

Focusing on Process and Product

Educational organizations are so structured that they tend to make most of their decisions using one organizational model, the bureaucratic model. We believe the bureaucratic model is quite appropriate for most decisions that are made in educational organizations. However, there are many decisions for which the bureaucratic model is not as appropriate as are other organization models.

In considering what is an appropriate model for making various types of decisions, there are two primary concerns. One deals with the *process* to be employed in making the decision, the other with the *product* that is to result from the process. A simple example comes from the automobile industry—the process is what is done to produce the car, and the car itself is the product.

The extent to which process is known and agreed on, or unknown and not agreed on, and the extent to which product is known and agreed on, or unknown and not agreed on dictates the kind of organization that can be most effective for making decisions.

Let us look at four different situations. (1) When process is known and/or agreed on and product is known and/or agreed on, the bureaucratic organization appears to be the most effective for decision-making. (2) When process is unknown and/or not agreed on and product is known and agreed on, a professional organization seems to be the most effective. (3) When process is known and/or agreed on and product is unknown and/or not agreed on, the collegial-deliberative organization seems to be the most effective for decision-making. And (4) when neither process nor product is known and/or agreed on, a state of anomie exists within the organization: very little will get done in the way of decision-making unless by fiat, consensus, or some other form of agreement on process and/or product.

We will now examine a hypothetical example so that the reader may better understand these different kinds of decision-making situations.

A new college has been established and has just admitted 300 freshmen who will be coming to campus in September, and it is now June. Faculty, administration, and staff are organized into a collegial-deliberative body to make the decisions that will establish the overall goals for learning of the incoming students. This type of organization is selected because at this time "product," or what the students are supposed to be at the end of four years, is not known and/or agreed on; though many feel that they *do* know, at least there is not general agreement on what these students should be at the end of four years. Thus there is a focus on *process* more than on the product—that is, on the process of making decisions about the overall goals of the organization. It is necessary to be as certain as possible that all the input needed for the highest quality decision-making is obtained and that all those who will implement the decisions are involved in making them to gain the highest level of acceptability. To meet these two basic aims, the focus must be on the process of deliberation, with rules and regulations governing how decisions will be made. (A good example outside education is the United States Congress. This organization cannot actually measure the product: the contented citizen. How much does the citizen want in terms of old-age pensions, health insurance, job security, and so on? The answers to these questions cannot be known and certainly cannot be agreed on; however, Congress *can* agree on how it will conduct its business, i.e., on the process for reaching its decisions, and it sets up careful rules, regulations, and procedures for reaching those decisions.)

One of the decisions made by the collegial-deliberative organization is that all the students will receive instruction that will increase their ability to communicate effectively. In achieving this goal, there are some rather obvious decisions where both process and product are known and/or generally agreed on. For example, we know that the students will have to meet somewhere with somebody, that they will require certain materials at certain times, that they will need instructions about where to meet and when, and that they will need some information about what is expected of them at what time, in what place, as judged by whom. We know that there will need to be a schedule and record-keeping—these certainly are usually agreed on and known as far as process and product are concerned, and hence lend themselves readily to the bureaucratic decision-making model.

The bookstore manager can proceed to arrange forms by which professors may order books and to set up whatever rules, regulations, and procedures he needs to ensure that the orders are properly processed, and that the books arrive, are checked in, and are dispensed efficiently. The registrar can set up whatever student accounting procedures are necessary to provide appropriate forms for reporting on class attendance, grades, or registration. There will not always be agreement on the procedures, but when disagreement results, appeals can be made to those within the bureaucratic hierarchy. If such appeals do not result in a satisfactory remedy, the appellant may ask that the collegial-deliberative body review the bureaucratic action to determine its relevance to the stated goal or goals.

As the goal to help students communicate more effectively is implemented by the faculty, we move to the professional organization model for decision-making. Though the product is known—students who have learned to communicate more effectively—the process to reach this goal is not known, for students differ much in skills, attitudes, and abilities, as do faculty. Decision-making now has to be viewed as idiosyncratic, left very much to the judgement of individual faculty members. The focus moves to product as far as evaluation is concerned. Decisions about the effectiveness of the efforts of professors is made by their colleagues and minimal attention is given to the process, or the means they employ for instruction.

There are different types of organizations for different kinds of decisions. Unfortunately, in educational organizations we rely much more than we should, considering the kinds of decisions we must make, on the bureaucratic model. When we know what it is we want to do and how to do it, the bureaucratic model is obviously appropriate. If we are less certain about or cannot agree on what it is we want done—in other words, the product or the result—the professional model is most appropriate and effective. This model provides for idiosyncratic behavior on the part of those who will produce the product and permits the use of imagination and creativity, not effectively provided for by either the bureaucratic or the collegial-deliberative model.

About the Operational Guides to Decision-Making

The next four chapters contain a series of operational guides to decision-making. They may be viewed as rules-of-thumb, general operating procedures that should be helpful to the decision-maker. They certainly are not gospel, but they can assist those charged with making decisions in educational organizations to view more realistically key variables affecting decisions they make.

The operational guides are in four categories. Each of the four categories is presented in a separate chapter, along with appropriate cases for study and discussion. Though the guides contribute to understanding the cases that appear in the chapter with them, one should not assume that operational guides appearing in other chapters would not also contribute to a better understanding of each case.

The operational guides in Category One constitute the premise on which all the other guides are based. (In fact, the two guides in chapter 5 constitute a premise for this entire book.) At the risk of oversimplification, this premise instructs the decision-maker to take the rational and logical acts and pronouncements of organizations seriously, but it cautions the reader not to take them too seriously. The two cases in chapter 5 that illustrate this premise are not actual cases. Our readers will quickly discover that they were written tongue in cheek, because the authors believe that the best way to illustrate the foibles of human beings convinced that they are acting with absolute rationality is to accept their rational statements and extrapolate them to the point where they become irrational.

The operational guides in Category Two present a constellation of the kinds of decisions one makes in organizations. Our thesis is that all decisions fall within one of the three operational guides presented. Obviously, the cases in chapter 6 are best understood by finding the appropriate operational guides.

The guides in Category Three focus on personal values and their impact on one's decisions. They are basically designed to help the reader clarify his primary values and his operational hierarchy for those values. We stress that the decision-maker's value hierarchy is the prime factor in how he will view a problem and then formulate his solution for it.

Category Four deals with more effective ways to behave in organizations to bring about change or to minimize resistance to what you want to do. These guides focus particularly on more effective ways to behave within bureaucratic organizations.

As the reader studies the operational guides he should apply them to the cases. He is encouraged to develop his own operational guides, for we have certainly not exhausted the universe of guides that are practical and helpful in understanding decision-making in educational organizations. Too few decision-makers think through those premises on which they base most of their decisions. The reader may well not care to accept the operational guides we set forth. This will be all to the good, if he follows his rejection of our guides with a systematic construction of some of his own.

With the exception of the two cases in chapter 5, all of the cases are taken from actual experiences of the authors, or of people known to one or both of the authors. Obviously, names and places have been disguised, but readers may feel that they have been in quite similar situations, for the cases were selected to include the entire range of decisions that are made in educational organizations. They are not confined to the classroom, the dean's office, the principal's office, or the president's office. We realize that many readers of this book may not expect to or want to be administrators at the president, principal, or dean level; however, we believe that one can understand better the decisions he may be called on to make—no matter what his place in the organization—if he has experienced even vicariously the kinds of decisions others in the organization are called on to make. One may often gain significant insight into his basic assumptions and his value hierarchy by analyzing cases that are not within his realm of experience and with which he cannot immediately identify.

When this book is used as a text, it is suggested that students analyze and then discuss the cases. Once certain points of view have been presented and argued, students should assume various roles and play those roles in the cases they have discussed. The results of these two activities back-to-back are sometimes startling, since the purely intellective, analytical "solutions" often differ dramatically from the "solutions" which role-playing produces. This phenomenon, we believe, further illustrates the validity of those operational guides in Category One that stress the ostensible rationality of organizations, but then cautions that rationality in actual practice is but one dimension of decision-making.

Notes for Part 2

1. William Ebenstein, *Today's Isms* (Englewood Cliffs, N.J.: Prentice-Hall, 1964), p. 135.

(5)

Category One: A Premise

The operational guides in Category One focus on the rationality of people in organizations and on their interpretations of reality or truth. These guides caution the reader about accepting at face value the assumptions made by people in organizations about what is real, true, logical, and rational. While we do not advocate irrational behavior in organizations, we do propose that there is effective behavior that is neither irrational nor rational, but rather intuitive. We accept the need for rationality in organizations, and assume that most people within them usually behave rationally, but we often view with considerable skepticism supposedly rational pronouncements that go against what our experience and intuition dictate to be inconsistent with stated goals or the organization.

The two cases in this chapter—which we would caution the reader are written tongue-in-cheek—illustrate what can happen in educational organizations when a given assumption is accepted blindly, then rationally and logically programmed to produce a self-fulfilling prophecy.

A quotation from Saint Anselm succinctly captures the essence of the two operational guides in Category One: "For I do not seek to understand that I may believe, but I believe in order to understand. For this I believe—that unless I believe—I should not understand."

Operational Guide 1

When a person says that something is true he means that it is true by virtue of (1) faith, (2) definition, (3) statistics, or (4) consensus.

In the decision-making process we continually encounter judgments as to whether something is true or valid. It is useful to place such judgments in some kind of analytic framework to see how the judge has reached his conclusion.

Many conclusions are *assertions of belief or faith.* "There *is* a God," declares one believer. In schools one often hears words to the effect that "if children are to perform well they need to be disciplined." In education one of the fundamental beliefs is that schools (a term that people use when they think of formal education) educate. This fundamental belief appeals to man's romantic self, for one could argue equally well that schools miseducate.

Some judgments are based on *truth by definition,* for example: "The student must read in order to graduate from college." Since the student must be able to read by the time he enters college, it is by definition true that he must be able to read to graduate from college. Truth by definition is an example of self-fulfilling prophecy; something "is true" because it is treated as true.

Statistical validity is a third form of reasoning done by proponents of a point of view. "If you turn on the ignition of the car it will probably start." "If a thoroughbred horse and a mule are in a race, the horse will probably win." An example from education might be: "Students who don't read at grade level by third grade probably will not read at grade level in the twelfth grade."

Finally, there is *truth by consensus.* A group of people agree on a given subject in order to get something done. For example, it is assumed by consensus that teachers are the best judges of a student's performance in the courses they teach. It is generally agreed that school should begin at a designated time and end at a designated time. Truth by consensus is invoked to lend stability and predictability to organizations.

As you, the reader and decision-maker, go through the decision-making exercises in this book, we hope you will be aware of the various bases for making judgments as to the validity of ideas. You should be aware of which type of "truth" you are accepting as a given when you make your decisions.

Operational Guide 2

Organizations point to rationality as the cement that holds them together, but in reality belief or faith holds them together.

Words tend to be self-serving, and organizational terms are no exception. Organizations use a rationalistic symbol system to convince the public and themselves that what they are doing is primarily rational. A simple example from our legal system illustrates this. Our court system is based on the three basic beliefs that courts (1) dispense justice, (2) determine the truth, and (3) determine the law through interpretation. If you accept all three of these beliefs, reason and rationality appear to be the cement that holds our court system together; if you delete any one of them, the system is rent asunder.

There are many similar examples in our system of formal education. Let us examine three basic beliefs on the sequencing of courses. First, it is commonly believed that a series of discrete courses taught in a certain sequence makes a person better educated. There is also a certain faith that the person who does well in going through the sequence is better educated than the person who does not. (Even finer distinctions are made, so that the person who has a 3.5 grade point average is considered better educated than the person who has a 2.5.) Finally, there is the belief that the professor or teacher evaluates the student who goes through the sequence of courses; it is assumed that this occurs after the professor has wisely selected both the material to be taught and the strategies for teaching such material.

What are the advantages to the educational decision-maker in realizing that faith rather than rationality is the cement that holds organizations together? The primary advantage is that the decision-maker learns to give attention to first assumptions; the logic of the system is less important than the initial premises adopted largely on the basis of faith. Secondly, one soon learns that rationality has limits in defending an idea or point of view. "You can't graduate because you have a 1.9 rather than a 2 point grade average" is an inadequate defense. "It is necessary to have cutoff points in order to make decisions, and our particular cutoff point is 2" is an adequate defense initially, for it argues for cutoff points rather than *a* particular cutoff point. If you try to find rationality and consistency in every decision within an organization you quickly become very anxious. Details of little significance seem to jump out as you are engaged in the decision-making process.

One learns to question what appears to be consistent and rational, for rationality and consistency do not in themselves determine "goodness." "Goodness" is a value assertion on the part of one who has faith in certain basic assumptions.

Case Study 1. "None Need Fail": A Model Guidance Program

B.F.S., Director of Guidance
Beauvoire High School

Our Guidance Program grew out of the cooperative effort of teachers, administrators, and counselors who adopted as a basic goal: "None need fail." To achieve this goal all recognized that it would be necessary to require of each student scholastic performance commensurate with his abilities and motives, to confront him with a curriculum challenging yet not overwhelming. Our staff concluded that such attention to individual needs could only be accomplished by a comprehensive educational plan that would include provision for aptitude and achievement testing, academic ability grouping, parent education, teacher cooperation, and an extensive counseling program. This paper describes the Guidance Program designed to achieve our goal: "None need fail."

Aptitude and achievement testing at Beauvoire complements the testing program of the junior high school that prepares our students. Tests are administered twice a year, in January and in June. Their results along with teacher and counselor evaluations and course grades enable us to evaluate student ability in relation to student performance, and to place students in appropriate academic ability groups.

The five academic ability groups at Beauvoire are: Honors, College Prep I, College Prep II, Standard, and Opportunity. Students entering as freshmen normally continue in the ability group in which they were enrolled in junior high school, since the high school curricula have as prerequisites subject matter included in the junior high curricula. (Junior high ability groups are similar in title and design to those found in the high school. For example, Honors mathematics at Beauvoire requires a background in basic algebra, which is included in the content of the Honors mathematics course in the Junior High School.) A brief description of the academic ability group follows:

(1) *Honors* provides a high level academic program for the outstanding college-bound student. Courses in the senior year are typically the equivalent of college freshmen courses. Students may enroll by invitation only in one but no more than four Honors courses.

(2) *College Prep 1* provides a college preparatory course designed to meet the admissions standards of the "typical selective" admissions college. Students are admitted on the basis of their ability to do a competent scholastic job and their declared intention of attending college.

(3) *College Prep 2* provides an adequate college preparation program for students to attend an "Open Door" college or a post-high school technical institute. Students are admitted on the basis of their ability to meet the standards of the program and their declared intention of continuing their education beyond high school.

(4) *Standard* provides a terminal education for the students preparing to work following graduation from high school. Vocational and/or business training, and general education comprise this program, and students are admitted if their abilities are sufficient to meet its standards.

(5) *Opportunity* provides a basic program for educables who cannot complete any of the four other programs. It enables the student to prepare himself for a productive life as a citizen.

Proper placement of students is crucial to the success of the Guidance Program; consequently much of the counselors' time is devoted to assessment of student abilities, interviews with parents, students, and teachers. At least twice each year records are reviewed, teachers consulted, parents and students interviewed—and often counseled—and decisions made about the efficacy of existing ability grouping.

No school program can succeed without optimum parental understanding, cooperation, and approval. We receive all in good measure from Beauvoire parents, but not without significant effort on our part. We have parent conferences during the summer preceding the student's freshman year, at which time we explain each student's academic strengths and weaknesses as related to the demands of our programs. Each parent is apprised of the importance of his child's need to succeed and assured that no child is permanently labeled by being placed in a particular ability group, that such placement is temporary and transfers are made when evidence supports them. Some parents are at first disappointed and need additional sessions with the counselor before recognizing the problems inherent in placing a child in an inappropriate ability group. Now and then a parent will insist that his child be placed in a given group despite the advice of counselor and teachers. If his wishes are not too unrealistic in the face of the evidence, his child is so placed, but counselor and teachers observe the child closely for indications of inability to "keep up." Often such indications are readily observed and the parents are apprised of their child's difficulties. They are in most cases then quite amenable to his being transferred to a more appropriate group.

Parents are encouraged to consult the counselor whenever they desire additional information about their child's progress and its relation to his future plans. We stress the need for a realistic assessment of student ability relative to student (and parental) aspiration. We point out that three of our academic programs provide adequate background for college, that colleges differ in admission standards and levels of academic difficulty, and that consequently high school programs must vary in standards, selection, and grading if they are to provide pre-college education. By this time test scores, grades, teacher evaluations, and student counseling sessions provide adequate evidence for predicting the probable success of a student both in a given ability group and in a given college.

Teacher cooperation is as essential as parental cooperation to the success of any school program, so our Guidance Program was planned cooperatively with the teachers. They saw the need for ability grouping but were concerned about the effects on grading, academic standards, and pupil attitudes. Consensus was reached on these two policies that guide our actions today: (1) weighting of grades and (2) different standards and content for the five ability groups. Grades are weighted according to the level of course difficulty, so that an A in an Honors course counts for five times as much as an A in an Opportunity course. A C in an Honors course is equivalent to an A in a College Prep 2 Course or to a B in a College Prep 1 course. Weighting grades in this manner enables us to make class an accurate index of student ability and achievement. A course at any ability level now relates directly to the preceding one and is a prerequisite for the course following it. Teachers do not need to compare what College Prep 1 students learn with what Honors students learn. They are free to plan their courses with the abilities of their own students in mind, to set standards relevant to those abilities and grade accordingly.

Of course, all is not ideal. Our counselors do encounter such problems as the "overachiever," the "underachiever," and the "behavior deviant." The overachiever is a student who is performing at present well beyond his basic ability; we try to show him that he may be "riding for a fall" if he expects to achieve at his present rate in the face of an increasingly rigorous academic challenge. The underachiever is achieving less than his ability warrants; we counsel him to ascertain the reasons for his poor achievement. Often we find that he has problems at home, with a teacher, or with his fellow students; we help him work out his own solutions, and when necessary refer him to the school psychologist or social worker. The behavior deviant is constantly in trouble with school rules and authority; we counsel him in an effort to help him recognize his problems so that he may seek solutions to them. All our counseling is predicated on the basis of the student's voluntary participation. Over the years, as the students have come to see the relation of counseling to the overall school program, and as they have come to recognize that we can help them, we have experienced little reluctance on their part to seek our help.

The reader should not conclude that we categorize our problems or prescribe their solutions on the basis of this too brief description of them. We recognize the individuality of each student; the success of our Guidance Program attests to this, for students, parents, and teachers would hardly support it as they do if they did not believe that the interests of each student were being served. Our students come to us because we do see them as individuals.

What evidence, other than parent and teacher support, do we have to indicate the merit of our Guidance Program?

(1) During the last three years no student recommended by our staff for admission to a college has been denied admission.

(2) Conversely, with the exception of "Open Door" colleges, no student not recommended has gained admission.

(3) With few exceptions (three in a four-year period), students who attended college without our recommendation did not complete the freshman year. (We are ambivalent about the meaning of this statistic. We believe it indicates the accuracy of our assessment of student ability but we are chagrined at the disappointment of the student and his parents.)

(4) Students attending college have increased their "staying power" markedly—from 64 percent to the present 89 percent over a ten-year period. (This at a time when the number of students attending college from Beauvoire has risen from 61 percent to 84 percent of the graduating class.)

(5) For the past two years no student at Beauvoire has experienced academic failure.

We take pride in this objective evidence of the success of our program, but the following letter from one of our recent graduates is the most gratifying endorsement of its success:

Dear Dr.________________:

These first two years of college have really shown me how lucky I was to have attended Beauvoire. During my freshman year here, while many of my classmates were frenetically chasing from course of study to course of study, insecure and uncertain of their reasons for being at college anyway, I was able to select a course of study which logically follows what I had studied in high school and relates directly to the career I shall follow upon graduation from college. Hence, college is a necessary and rational "bridge" between high school and vocational objective.

Thanks to the preparation I received at Beauvoire, I have been able to avoid much useless expenditure of time and energy trying this course and that. I have been able to concentrate on what I needed to do, because I knew what I could and in turn wanted to do.

Two years from now I will have my degree and my teaching certificate. Hopefully three years from that time I will have completed my requirements for a counselor's certificate. Wouldn't it be fitting for me to return to Beauvoire as a member of the counseling staff?

Gratefully,

H. G. W.

Case Study 2. How to Rate a College

Today's high school graduate faces a bewildering task in selecting a college. He knows that colleges differ in admission standards, costs, social environment, and, most important, in the quality of education offered. He can find out about admission standards, costs, and the social environment. But, while he knows colleges differ in quality of education, he can't find out how and how much. He is reduced to accepting testimonials from the college's alumni and students, or from its admissions representative. Instead of testimonials he needs hard answers to such questions as: Is education at a state college superior to that at a private college? Is a Yale degree better than a Harvard degree? Does Berea offer a course study more demanding than Campbellville's? These questions can be answered if a quantitative scale or rating device is developed that can measure what is taught and how well.

It is a truism that a college is its faculty. It can be no better or worse than the professors who staff it. What is taught and how well it is taught are questions of who teaches. Once we can make valid judgments about the quality of a faculty we can make valid judgments about the quality of a college. The task then is to develop a scale that will systematically measure the worth of the professor.

What are the characteristics of professorial excellence and how can they be measured? To determine those characteristics, look to those who can make basic decisions based on a knowledge of professorial excellence: college administrators, and professors themselves. They decide matters of tenure, salary increases, and promotion by weighing the merit of a man's achievement in teaching, research, and publications.

In teaching, judgments are made on the basis of the academic level of students taught and the number of students taught. The most esteemed professors teach the most advanced students and the more advanced students are enrolled in the smallest classes. A college recognizes excellence in teaching by assigning the best professors to teach the most advanced students in the smallest classes.

A professor's research is judged by his peers as well as by the administration, according to its "purity" and the extent of its funding. The "purity" of research is decreed by those prominent in the field in which the research is undertaken. The "purer" it is, the more likely it is to be comprehended only by the most advanced minds in the field; also, the less likely it is to have immediate applicability to the resolution of current human problems. (Another factor of "purity," particularly in the social sciences, is a geographical one. Research done in a foreign country is usually "purer" than that done at home.)

The degree to which research is funded is evidence of its merit. When research is paid for by outside sources, foundations, industry, and government, its value is obvious. The professor conducting it is rewarded by promotion, and a lighter teaching load.

No one denies that good professors publish, but the fact of publication does not ensure professorial excellence in writing. What he publishes must be in his own field of scholarship. Its value can be assessed by determining who reads it and who publishes it. A book or article that is "popularized" and read by a large portion of the public is of dubious scholarly quality. The work of Rhine and Kinsey may be exceptions, but many scholars in psychology and biology do not believe so. On the other hand, a publication read by a select group of recognized scholars in a field is probably high in scholarship, for who publishes a book or article is, of course, closely related to who reads it. Articles published by popular magazines or books published by commercial presses are not likely to be scholarly. Articles published by professional journals or books published by university presses probably are.

Having identified the criteria used by colleges to rate their faculties, it is possible to develop a rating scale that will uniformly measure the quality of professors at any college.

The Nelson Scale for rating college professors is such a scale, though admittedly at this stage of its development a primitive one. Through extensive use it can be refined, additional criteria added, and measurement of criteria made more accurate.

The Nelson Scale assigns points for the quality of professors' teaching, research, and publications. It provides a quantitative basis for judging their competence. Once a college, using the Nelson Scale, measures the worth of its faculty it will have valid evidence of the quality of education it offers.

The formula $\frac{\Sigma P}{N} = Q$ yields a quality rating for a college where
ΣP = Total rating of all professors,
N = Number of faculty,
Q = Quality of education at the college.

The Nelson Scale for Rating College Professors

I. Quality of Teaching

A. Academic level of students taught

Freshmen and Sophomores	0 points
Juniors and Seniors	1 point
Masters candidates only	2 points
Ph.D. candidates only	3 points
Postdoctoral students	4 points
No teaching but consults	5 points

[A bonus might be given if consulting is done primarily at other universities or with industry or government; a double bonus if consulting takes place outside the continental United States.]

B. Number of students taught per year

100 or more	0 points
75-98	1 point
50-74	2 points
25-49	3 points
1-24	4 points
0	5 points

II. Quality of Research

A. "Purity" of Research

Applied immediately to current human problems	0 points
Applied immediately to other academic disciplines	1 point
Not applied but understood by professors in other academic disciplines	2 points
Not applied but understood by junior scholars in discipline of the research	3 points
Not applied but understood by another professor in the discipline of research at the university.	4 points
Not applied and understood only by renowned scholars in the discipline of research at another university	5 points

B. Funding of Research

[Funds provide not only for basic costs of faculty doing research, but also pay for buildings, equipment, and support of three or more graduate students.]

Not funded	0 points
Funded partially by the university	1 point
Funded wholly by the university	2 points
Funded partially by sources outside the university	3 points
Funded wholly by sources outside the university	4 points
Funded wholly by outside sources	5 points

III. Quality of Publication

A. Readers of Publication

The general public	0 points
College graduates or equivalents	1 point
Holders of graduate degrees	2 points
Professors outside the discipline	3 points
Graduate students in the discipline (required reading)	4 points
Esteemed professors in the discipline	5 points

B. Published by

Popular magazine or commercial press	0 points
Textbook publishers (sells over 20,000 copies)	1 point
Textbook publishers (sells less than 20,000 copies)	2 points
Scholarly journal	3 points
University press	4 points
University press (distributed free to a select group of libraries)	5 points

The Nelson scale can be refined after experiences with its use. One possible refinement is that the scale take into consideration the time spent on campus by a professor. The more capable professors are often called to the service of industry and government, both foreign and domestic. The scale might provide zero points for a professor who was on campus each day school was in session and five points for a professor who was absent from the campus every day school was in session. Many other professorial attributes could be measured, each addition promoting the validity of the scale.

Once each college faculty has been rated and the ratings published, students will have reliable evidence for making decisions about the quality of education offered by a college. No institution will score 30+ points, tops on the Nelson Scale. There simply are not that many talented men available, but many of the better known eastern, midwestern, and far western universities may well score twenty or above.

Students seeking the best will look for universities in the 20-to-30 point range, while students who must settle for less than the best will look for colleges scoring below 20. Poorer students can hope to be accepted only by colleges scoring 12 or below.

Conclusion

Our goal in this chapter has been to demonstrate the limitations of rationality in the decision-making process. The rhetoric used in the rational process is self-serving when accepted at face value by the educational decision-maker. We hasten to add that we have not adopted a position that is opposed to rationality, but instead argue that there must be a balance between rationality, intuition, and previous experiences of the decision-maker.

(6)

Category Two: A Decision-Making Constellation

The operational guides in Category Two constitute a constellation within which all educational decisions fall. The three operational guides in Category Two should help the reader recognize that most decisions are relative. There are not good decisions or bad decisions, there are only decisions that are more appropriate for one situation than for another.

We use the terms *good* and *bad* two dimensionally—in terms of good for the individual as reflected in his own value hierarchy, and in terms of effectiveness as far as the organizational operation is concerned. The decision-maker certainly should be alert to the fact that "good" in terms of his own values is often not the same as effectiveness of organizational operation. The cases that follow the operational guides certainly should bring that point home.

Operational Guide 3

Many decision-making situations place the decision-maker in the position of choosing from several good alternatives.

Western culture teaches us to think in terms of extremes. One goes to heaven or hell, one follows God or the devil, and one has to choose between the good and the bad, right and wrong. To think in terms of extremes provides us with a sense of security, for everything can be categorized quickly into one of two camps. One would think that a fast-moving, technologically advanced society would lend itself to seeing things in terms of degrees of differences rather than extremes. However, a common reaction to a more complex, accelerated situation is to revert to simple methods for classifying what we experience. Furthermore, such classifications are not only used to describe but become simple moral judgments as to how one should behave in the future. For example, it is but a small step from describing people as good or bad to saying that the type of people being described will always be good and their opposite will always be bad. The stereotype is set. We also know that technological advances can be used to set stereotypes rather than to educate people to accept differences. Television, radio, motion pictures, and mass meetings can be used to serve any purpose.

It naturally follows that as decision-makers we often think in terms of extremes. "I have to choose between a good alternative and a bad one, a right choice and a wrong one." The truth is that this does not apply to most decision-making situations. Instead, the choice is from among several good alternatives, so that the challenge is to support what we think is the best possibility at the time.

A concrete example will illustrate what we mean. As a parent with three young children, you value the following "goods": the child's freedom to develop as an individual; the child's safety; your own life-style. Each of these is obviously worthwhile. The question is not choosing between good and bad alternatives, but assigning priorities to three very good values. A dilemma occurs when one of your children, age five, wants to cross the street alone at any time he wishes. In your judgment as a parent, crossing at certain times in certain situations, such as when you or another older person is there, is safe. By setting this limitation you necessarily take some freedom away from the child in the interest of his safety, and take some freedom from yourself by obligating yourself to take him across the street when you would prefer to be doing something else. A course of action designed to give total satisfaction to all three "goods" is obviously impossible.

Looking at the same situation in extreme terms, one might reason as follows: "My choice is between freedom for the child, safety of the child, and my own life-style. As soon as I select one of these as *the* good the other two are necessarily categorized as bad. If I select my life-style as good, then the child's freedom and safety are 'bad.' That is, whenever the child's freedom and safety conflict with my life-style, they will have to be sacrificed. It's all or none." If we examine the way many parents live, we can see that in fact their decision to make their own life-style paramount, to the exclusion or subjugation of the other two "goods," does make a difference in the child's life—in this case to the child's freedom and safety. Some parents feel that their children interfere with their life-style of staying out late many nights during the week. In fact, the child's safety and freedom are threatened by this.

The parent's view that two factors—the child's safety and the child's freedom—are bad or evil, means that they will accommodate such factors only in times of great pressure. For example, when the child's freedom is limited to the point where he becomes openly rebellious, this then is a greater threat to the parents' life-style than are minor concessions to his freedom. The child, not allowed at any time to cross the street, can resort to temper tantrums or be constantly irritating to his parents to the point where the parents' life-style is threatened more than can be resolved simply by taking the child across the street on limited occasions. The parent gives in, feeling frustrated, guilt-ridden, and probably hostile. The child has learned that the best way to get his way is to threaten the parents' life-style through confrontation. Confrontation thereby becomes a normal avenue of communication between child and parent.

Most peoples' views of large organizations support the extremist position: management is good, labor is bad; or labor is good, management is bad. Some leaders and negotiators in organizations know that this kind of simplistic thinking is reserved for public relations purposes. Others, however, do see themselves in "white hats" and the opposition in "black hats."

Let us now turn to a large organization and see how the attitude toward decision-making that we have advocated can make a difference. Two main "goods" are valued operationally by the military: efficiency as evidenced in winning battles; and support of United States foreign policy and relationships with other governments dictated by such policy. Particular decision-making situations require that both these goods must be accommodated, which means that neither will be completely maximized or achieved. For example, Country X is involved in military action in support of Country Y against a neighboring country, W, which in the judgments of leaders of the United States benefits our country's foreign relations with both Countries X and Y. The United States government feels that the most efficient way to deal with enemy W of Countries X and Y is literally to "wipe it off the map" with six hydrogen bombs. Yet in doing this our foreign relations with Countries A, B, and C would deteriorate to the point where they and other nations would break off relations with the United States. Countries D and E might also go to war with the United States as a result of treatment of the neighbor of Countries X and Y. A compromise is made between two "goods": military efficiency is achieved to a degree, by the offer of military aid, but not to the point where foreign relations with other countries will be seriously impaired.

A simplistic, extremist view of the same matter would be that military efficiency is good and anything that interferes with it, including foreign relations, is bad. Foreign relations would then only be considered when diplomatic concessions would aid military efficiency. For example, a country would be destroyed unless it could be demonstrated that such action would result in losing an ally essential to continued military efficiency.

As educational decision-makers, we also make the mistake of thinking in extreme terms, failing to see that most decisions involve choosing from among several good alternatives. Today's teacher, for example, is deluged with teaching methods and materials that are in large measure a result of technological advancements and attention given to education in the post-Sputnik era. This means in fact that the teacher usually has a choice from among several good alternatives. She can use simulation games, sociodrama, various discussion techniques, multimedia devices, and the like. Yet we hear teachers say such things as "Simulation games are worthless" and "Movies are a waste of time." These remarks simply indicate that the teacher is thinking in terms of the good versus the bad. This certainly simplifies teaching, for all that is classified as "bad" does not even have to be considered for instruction, but both teachers and students suffer from such extremist thinking.

A high school English teacher was annoyed by a boy in the back of the room who had his feet on the desk. She felt that this threat to her authority meant that she could not teach English well. She placed a high priority on getting the student to remove his feet from the desk so that she could maintain her authority and teach English, and when she asked him to remove his feet from the desk and he failed to do so she saw the situation as a choice between a good (teaching English well) and a bad (challenge to her authority). She should have then seen this as a priority question.[1] Teaching English well was a good that should have been ranked above maintaining authority. She had in fact escalated the annoyance on her value hierarchy so that she could not proceed with her teaching unless the boy took his feet off the desk. The boy was equally stubborn, and the resulting confrontation seriously impaired the English lesson for all students. One alternative to her approach would have been to give low priority to the annoyance so that all students could have profited from the English lesson. The teacher should not have treated his having his feet on the desk as an annoyance, especially since other students did not seem to be influenced by the boy.

It is interesting to look at the words used to describe the kinds of situations in which decision-makers find themselves. Our choice of terms reflects basic attitudes toward human affairs. For example, we use the term "problem" in such a way that we assume that there is a solution to every problem. This lends itself to viewing some choices as good or right if they solve the problem, or bad or wrong if they do not. People constantly say that that was a good or bad decision or that a solution was right or wrong. A more realistic approach is to view human affairs as a series of dilemmas, not problems. A dilemma exists when one is faced with a choice from several good or desirable alternatives.

A problem situation exists when there is a conflict within a closed system. For example, the problem is to know what two and two add up to. By definition, a closed system, a base ten number system, dictates the answer: four. Few decision-making situations are so uncomplex. Instead they involve the decision-maker in dilemmas with no one solution, no right or wrong answer, no good or bad answer. How to best teach two plus two equals four serves as an example of a dilemma. Dilemmas are then reconciled rather than solved.

A much maligned word is "compromise." People use it in a closed system context as if they were compromising the right answer. As we use it "compromise" is a major device for reconciling dilemmas, a choice among several goods, whereby a particular good is enhanced but not to the point that other goods are jeopardized.

You probably now wonder, "What difference does looking at decision-making in terms of operational guide 3 make?" It makes a lot of difference in how you feel about yourself and in your ability to control what happens to you. If one is continually concerned as to whether a decision is bad or good, he lives in perpetual fear of making bad choices. He feels guilty for making a "bad" or "wrong" decision, and instead of devoting his energy to thinking positively of ways to make better decisions in the future, he wastes his energy feeling sorry for himself, apologizing, or finding excuses. He becomes more and more hesitant about making decisions and tries to avoid situations which require making decisions. He becomes a reactor rather than an actor, forever on the defensive and at the mercy of others as they decide for him.

If, on the other hand, one recognizes that decisions are not right or wrong, good or bad, he can live with life as it truly is—ambiguous. At the same time, he comes to realize that decision-making can make a difference, enhancing his self-confidence and self-concept. Realizing that there is no perfect solution or answer, one can be proud of having made a decision, for the faint-hearted can't; he can know his decision was made on the best information available at the time, and be assured that his involvement in future decision-making activities will be important. In short, he will feel better about his decisions.

Operational Guide 4

The decision-maker will necessarily do some things he believes he should not do and certainly prefers not to do. He should then choose what he considers the least harmful decision to himself and others.

The most extreme example of this guide is justifiable homicide. The subject is faced with two alternatives: being killed or killing. A man draws a gun on you saying "I'm going to kill you" and, armed yourself, you shoot him before he can shoot you. Neither alternative is a "good" one. You simply chose what was in your judgment at the moment the most justifiable alternative.[2]

A less extreme example concerns a young unwed mother. She identifies three main alternatives: she can marry the father although she does not love him; she can have an abortion; or she can bear an illegitimate child. Her choice depends on what she thinks is least harmful to herself and others, and what is most justifiable given the situation.

A television repairman is ordered by his employer to replace tubes which in the repairman's judgment do not need replacing. After some discussion, the employer admits that the tubes may not need replacing but still insists that the only way the company can show a reasonable profit is by "padding" bills. The employee has the following options: he can quit; he can defy the boss; or he can do as he was told. Once again, the decision-maker is forced to choose the least harmful and thus most justifiable option.

A newly graduated first year teacher is unhappy about the options open to her in evaluating student progress. It is school policy that grades are to be given. The school has traditionally used class norms for such gradings, which means that those who consistently receive low grades tend to have poor self-concepts. If the teacher must use grades, she would prefer to grade on individual progress with the aim of building self-confidence in all her students. To do this she would give special assignments tailored to the individual needs and differences of students. She knows that she will probably be criticized by the admininstration, teachers, and some students if she pursues this different kind of grading procedure. A more drastic option open to her is not to give grades, but this could very well cost her her job. Our first year teacher's options all have bad features; she must find the one that is least harmful to students and herself.

A more experienced teacher teaches in a school where corporal punishment is an accepted practice. She opposes the use of corporal punishment. She has a disruptive student who consistently misbehaves in class. If kept in the room he will probably continue to disrupt and may even get worse. She has considered putting him in the hall on occasion but it is against school policy to leave a child unattended. Her principal practices corporal punishment regularly. If she sends the disruptive student to the office, he will surely receive such punishment. All the alternatives have bad features, and she must choose the one that will be least harmful to the students and herself.

You will note that in the examples presented the decision-maker who makes use of guide 4 is usually in the role of reactor rather than actor. As a reactor, he does not have the control over the situation that the initiator-actor does, but must respond on the basis of limited alternatives. The reactor's challenge is to get maximum benefit from such alternatives. That is, he needs to have as much control over the situation as is possible.

There are ways to avoid being in the reactor role for any length of time, allowing you to take the initiative as soon as possible. The most obvious way is to quit or drop out hoping that your next position will give you greater opportunity to set your own stage—to control the variables.

There are, however, many other less drastic alternatives. Postponement is a common tactic used by the decision-maker in the reactor role. The reactor may form a committee, claim a more pressing matter, or leave town for a period of time to think about how he should react. Another common tactic is to disclaim responsibility for the controversial decision. The television repairman, for example, might say that he could do nothing about the company's policy on replacing tubes, and the teacher might say she had no part in creating the corporal punishment policy.

All these tactics can be effective at different times. Our point is that whenever and wherever possible the decision-maker should be the actor rather than the reactor, and when in the role of reactor the decision-maker must be honest with himself as to why he chose this or that alternative.

At this point, the reader might well ask, "What advantages will there be if I follow guide 4?" Like guide 3, its advantages are primarily psychological. The decision-makers in our examples need not feel guilty for deciding to do a "bad" or "wrong" thing, since they were faced with no single option that was "good"—free from harm or distaste. They were guided then by selecting the option that was least harmful or least distasteful from among options all of which were harmful and/or distasteful.

It is unrealistic to think that one never has to choose from among several distasteful or harmful courses of action. The decision-maker who thinks otherwise may rationalize a "bad" act by saying to himself, "I did it in order to achieve something good." The television repairman, for example, may reason as follows: "Overcharging for minor repairs is justifiable in order to reduce what may seem to be prohibitive costs for major repairs. To overcharge for a tube replacement will not cost any one customer too much; this will allow us to minimize costs for a total overhaul of other television sets whose high cost would force the customer to buy a new set." This kind of thinking is the basis for the insurance industry. In the writing of automobile insurance policies, the underwriter overcharges the 90 percent who are not likely to be involved in accidents.

A second way to rationalize a "bad" act is by saying that the act was "right" after all. Our television repairman, for example, may replace a working tube and justify doing so by thinking that the tube would probably have gone out three or four months later and the customer is saving a future service charge by replacing the tube now. The teacher may say that grading is practiced throughout life in some form, giving in to rationalization for what she considers to be a bad practice.

Operational Guide 5

Some decision-making situations involve balancing the desirable with the undesirable. Trade-offs are made so that you can get what you want with the minimum amount of concession to what you consider to be undesirable.

A recent graduate of a well-known university was anxious to begin her first full-time teaching experience. Armed with the most recent ideas about open classrooms, one of her main objectives was to teach in an exciting and innovative manner. During her days as a university student she wore miniskirts, maxiskirts, and experimented with various hair colors. During the last year of her university work, she, like many of her friends, adopted the braless look. In short, our recent graduate values innovation both in her personal life-style and in her teaching. The problem is that many of her colleagues and her rather conservative principal will find her innovative life-style to be quite annoying; innovative teaching could make it doubly annoying. She knows that if she dresses in a more traditional manner her innovative approach to teaching will probably have a much better chance of success. The recent graduate is faced with a dilemma and she must compromise somewhere in order to balance the "desirable" with the "undesirable." In a sense, she is faced with the question, "What do I believe in more?" We have used the term "dilemma" rather than "problem," since there is no easy answer to the situation in which she finds herself. The result that she settles on will never be totally satisfying for she was placed in a forced choice situation.

The challenge to the teacher as a decision-maker is to effect those compromises that make the minimum amount of concession to what is considered to be undesirable in the interest of achieving the desirable.

A first year teacher, accustomed to the relative freedom from constraints in the university setting, objected to having to fill out attendance forms, late-for-class forms, demerit forms, and the like. He decided to stop filling out forms, as he ranked freedom from such tasks very high in his value hierarchy. When it was discovered in the administrative office that one teacher was consciously not following bureaucratic procedures, a great deal of attention was paid to all behavior on the part of the delinquent teacher. His colleagues also criticized him for not doing his share in disciplining students. Any innovation he wanted to initiate was suspect and given a great deal of attention.

In our discussion thus far, we have indicated that compromise is an inevitable part of decision-making. This does not mean, however, that the decision-maker avoids risk-taking. The decision-maker must recognize that some decisions of the high gain type also carry high risks. As the decision-maker wants to maximize gain and minimize loss, high risk decisions should be reserved for rare occasions in which the potential gains to the organization are also high. The decision-maker who fails to reserve high risk decisions for rare occasions will soon find that he is not taken seriously, since all his decisions are extremist. He may well find that his job is in jeopardy since his behavior is judged to be erratic by his colleagues and bureaucratic superiors.

The following examples demonstrate how two teachers reserved high risk decisions for rare occasions:

A department chairman in a high school interviewed several candidates for a position in the department. Although the chairman was quite a young man, most members of the department were old and traditional in their approach to teaching. They supported candidates of a like nature. One of the candidates for a position was very bright and had excellent credentials, but he was quite outspoken and did not fear dealing with controversial issues. Although the department chairman knew the risk he was taking was high, he forwarded the recommendation that the bright but controversial candidate should be hired.

A fifth grade teacher was concerned about a student who was little liked by his fellow students. This boy was outspoken, teased others, especially the poor readers, and used a variety of techniques to gain attention in class. The teachers in the later elementary grades were asked to appoint a student from each room to serve on the student government organization. Feeling that the "problem student" might possibly gain a great deal from such a position, the teacher decided to appoint him as class representative. She did this in spite of the fact that such an appointment might reflect unfavorably on her and the class.

High risk decisions require the proper relationship between reasonableness and emotions for a given situation. Although one must be in control of his emotions, it is often advantageous to use emotions to convey the feelings of importance attached to that which the decision-maker is proposing. In short, emotions are persuasive techniques that the decision-maker can use in order to:

(1) Draw attention to the importance of the matter at hand;
(2) Indicate that the time for action has come;
(3) Bring the people in the organization to focus on the issue you wish to focus on; and
(4) Draw people's attention to the weaknesses of measures you oppose.

What the decision-maker does when he deals with others on an emotional level is to make the milieu less predictable with respect to personal and organizational relationships. As such, the use of emotions is risky and can backfire by creating an emotional reaction of equal or greater intensity, as indicated in the following dialogue between a teacher and his principal:

Teacher: I'm interested in your impressions of the direction in which our math department is moving.

Principal: They say they're teaching the new math but it looks to me as if they're simply doing many of the same things. The least they can do is to be honest about what they're doing. (All said in an unemotional, straight-forward language)

Teacher: Wait a minute! Some of my best friends are in math! When you say they're being dishonest, you really need to give evidence! (Emotional)

Principal: I don't think you really mean that! Why do you take this so personally? (Emotional)

Emotions can also be overused, with the result that they lose their effect on others. What often happens is that colleagues and others isolate the person they consider to be too emotional, for his or her behavior is unpredictable.

There are times when the decision-maker should defer making a decision until more favorable circumstances arise. Although the decision-maker feels that something ought to be done, it may mean accommodating something that he doesn't think should be done. If what he thinks shouldn't be done is significant enough, he should do nothing for the moment and hope for a better decision-making situation in the future.

A schoolteacher has been annoyed in recent weeks by a boy who seems to resent her authority in the classroom. The boy has talked back, sworn in class, and teased the boy sitting next to him a great deal. The teacher's first reaction was to punish the boy in a variety of ways in order to keep him in line. Yet she reconsiders immediate action for she intuits that the boy is under pressure from some other source—possibly at home. She therefore decides to do nothing at the time hoping for more data and a more favorable decision-making situation in the future.

Near the end of the school year, the high school administration and several teachers are faced with a difficult situation. Ten juniors and fifteen seniors took a field trip on a school bus. Two of the twenty-five students reported to a counselor that marijuana was smoked on the bus by two juniors and three seniors. The principal called a meeting of the teachers who had the five accused students in their classes. This group of people decided to make no decision largely because of the lateness of the school year and the question of what constitutes evidence in such a case.

The main advantage of "balancing the desirable with the undesirable" is pragmatic: the decision-maker plays the odds and gets something, a part of what he ideally wants, instead of being engaged in an all-or-none operation. Some decision-makers seem to be waiting in anticipation of an ideal decision-making situation. The person who practices the present postulate places himself in the role of the pragmatist rather than of the idealist. The decision-maker realizes that compromise is inevitable when two or more people get together. The extreme idealist feels guilty when he is forced to compromise, and his guilt feelings get in the way of effective decision-making. The idealist's position is that of an absolutist. Compromise to many is a dirty word, whereas it is in fact sine qua non for people with different goals being able to work together. The English teacher who wants time for the senior play dress rehearsal to be taken out of class time must be willing to reciprocate in some way when others want to take students out of her class.

Case Study 1

President Batte was awakened by the jangling of the phone. The alarm clock on the night stand showed 2:30 a.m. Mumbling a sleepy "hello," he listened as the senior dorm counselor at the McIntosh Dorm excitedly blurted out, "The police and fire departments are here and have evacuated the dorm and won't let anybody back in unless you take full responsibility. There were two calls to the police station that bombs had been planted in the dorm, and the firemen and police came and got everybody out. As you know, it's about 10 degrees outside and I've tried to get the students into other dorms but we've just had two more bomb threats in Sallinger and Smith Dorms, and the police are ready to evacuate them. Captain Jonas of the police department is here and wants to talk to you. Here's the phone, Captain Jonas."

"Captain Jonas, here. President Batte, what do you want us to do?"

Case Study 2

The phone rang just as President Batte was sitting down to dinner. His daughter Debby answered, and told him that Senator Johnson, chairman of the Joint Legislative Finance Committee, wanted to speak to him. Picking up the phone, Batte said, "Hello Mike, what's the news?"

Johnson replied, "John, I think I can get you another 2.5 million dollars for building if you can spend it the way some of the members of the committee think it should be spent. Let me brief you, but first let me say that I think you'd better get over here if you can. I can hold off for a couple of hours, and it would take you about an hour and a half to drive over. While you're driving you might think about these things because I'll need an answer by the time you get here. I know that you definitely want two new buildings this time, the new physics building and the new social science building, and they are top priority on your building list. Down the list, of course, comes the library addition, the computer center, the administration building, and finally the Astroturf, new dressing rooms, and increased seating approval for the physics building. There is 2.5 million more available to be allocated for building at either your place or at Jackson University. Jackson's representatives are making a good case, but I think I can hold the money for you if you'll accent it for upgrading the athletic facilities. I am sure I can't get it for anything else."

"O.K., Mike," Batte responded. "I'll think about it. I'm leaving now. Will see you in about an hour and a half."

As he pulled into the parking lot at the state capitol, Batte was still not certain what his answer should be. In his judgment athletic facilities were a very low priority. Also, the priority list for buildings had been developed after much study by a committee composed of faculty, students, and administrators. As he walked up the steps of the capitol he was met by Senator Johnson who asked, "Well, John, what do I tell them?"

Case Study 3

Walt Wash, dean of the School of Education, had just returned from a conference with the academic vice-president of the university. In that conference they had discussed the problem of promotion for two assistant professors holding faculty rank in the School of Education, but who were spending three-fourths of their time in administration at the central university level. The two young men were apparently exceptionally able administrators. They had been at the university for six years, one as the associate dean of admissions, and the other as the assistant dean of the graduate school. Each taught one course in the School of Education, and from all reports each did a satisfactory teaching job. Neither had published during his tenure, and neither was greatly involved in the activities of the School of Education since their administrative responsibilities took most of their working day.

The vice-president had indicated to Walsh that he and the president felt strongly that these two men should be considered for promotion, and that appropriate procedures should be initiated in the School of Education to recommend them to the president for promotion.

Walsh knew that the publications record and general service to the School of Education of the two men would not merit promotion. He also knew that his senior professors would not view favorably academic promotion based on performance in central administrative roles.

The policy statement concerning promotion at the university was as follows: "Recommendations for promotion will be made by the Dean of the School after consultation with an appropriate faculty committee, such committee to include at least fifty percent faculty holding the rank of professor. Recommendations for promotion will be made to the academic Vice President, who will then recommend those he deems worthy to the President."

It was now January 7, and Walsh had called a meeting of his promotions committee for February 10. It was his custom to recommend worthy faculty for promotion and to encourage recommendations from all faculty in the school. He had not, prior to his conversation with the vice-president, planned to recommend the two assistant professors assigned to central administration.

Case Study 4

The women who worked in the school cafeteria had an unwritten rule that they verbally communicated to students: "If you buy two hot dogs you have to eat both of them yourself." Since the first hot dog was 24 cents and the second was 10 cents many students didn't buy lunch but instead bought a hot dog from a friend for 10 cents. This practice made the cafeteria workers angry. On two occasions the cooks grabbed half-eaten hot dogs out of the mouths of students who hadn't purchased their own lunches, stalked to the nearest wastebaskets with the hot dogs, and dropped them in.

Students who witnessed these incidents in the cafeteria brought the cooks' actions to the attention of Jim Sands, a new teacher in the school. Jim talked to the principal, but it was clear that the latter was unwilling to interfere with cafeteria affairs.

Jim Sands reported his conversation with the principal to the students who made the initial inquiry. When asked what to do at this point, he recommended that the students take their grievance to the student government. The student government's inaction further angered some students. The cooks, aware of the controversy, decided to dig in and hold their ground. The head cook was so outraged at one of the student s "insolence" in the cafeteria line that she dumped his whole tray into the dishwasher's tub. This incident incensed the majority of the students and they organized a very effective boycott of the cafeteria.

Soon after the boycott began, the principal stormed into Jim Sands' room during his planning period. "What do you think you're doing? You started this whole mess! Now we'll probably lose our federal food subsidy for the cafeteria!"

Case Study 5

Nine o'clock Monday morning, President John Batte III was at his desk reading the morning's mail. The door to his office opened and his assistant, Bill Smith, entered and said, "All hell is breaking loose on the building site of the new library."

President Batte asked, "What's going on?"

Smith replied, "Well, you know they are beginning construction on the new library today, and for the past two months while no work was being done students have been parking their cars on the libary site. When the construction crews got there this morning they weren't able to get to work, and the campus director of security called two wreckers and began to tow the cars away. A crowd of students gathered and blocked the wreckers' path. Now the students are lifting up the compact cars and setting them in the street. The city police have been called and probably are already there. I think there must be at least a thousand students surrounding the library site, and they certainly are in an ugly mood."

Case Study 6

Soon after assuming the presidency of Elgin University, Walter Parker realized that the athletic program of the university was in serious difficulty. He had heard some rumors before accepting the presidency, but the rumors had not even touched the surface of the major problems facing the university's athletic program. There was more than enough evidence to indicate that in at least three of the sports at the university many violations of conference and NCAA rules and regulations had taken place. At his first meeting with the presidents of the other conference schools Parker had been shown incontrovertible evidence of a series of violations on the part of coaches, assistant coaches, and alumni at Elgin, any one of which would have been sufficient for suspension of the university from the conference and for probation of the university by the NCAA. Parker promised the council of presidents that he would immediately set up an investigating committee and, once all the facts were gathered, take appropriate action against the responsible parties and make a full report to the conference on the investigation and the actions ensuing from it.

Returning to campus, Parker immediately convened the University Athletic Committee and acquainted them with some of the problems. He requested that a blue ribbon committee be appointed to do a thorough investigation of the athletic program at Elgin. The committee was appointed and met twice a week for six weeks. At this point the chairman indicated in a conversation with Parker that the committee would complete its study in another four weeks, and also indicated that all members of the committee were thoroughly shocked at the state of affairs in the university's athletic department.

On Friday morning Parker was clearing up some matters in his office before leaving to catch a plane to attend the meeting of the presidents of the conference schools. It was Parker's intention at that meeting to tell the presidents that he expected a final report from the investigating committee in four weeks, and that a copy of that report would be sent to all the presidents before the final meeting of the council, which was to take place in May. Parker also intended to report that all funds used by the athletic department were being screened by a special assistant to the president who was also monitoring the activities of the coaches and assistant coaches.

As he was about to leave the office his secretary told him that the university vice-president for business was on the line. Parker picked up the phone and was told by the vice-president that there was an emergency matter that he needed to talk to Parker about immediately. Parker told him to come over but that the conference would need to be a quick one since his plane left in an hour and fifteen minutes, and it was a thirty-minute drive to the airport.

Once seated in the office, Vice-President Svenson began, "You recall that $250,000 furniture order we had for the new dormitory? Well, it's just started to come in and I find that none of the styles we ordered are included. In fact we've been given furniture that is inferior in quality, but the price seems to be the same as the price of the furniture we ordered. I've called the state director of purchasing, and he contends that the furniture is of equal quality, and that it is his prerogative to make such judgments and that we have no choice but to accept the furniture. I've told the delivery people to stop unloading the furniture since it's not what we ordered and we have no intention of accepting responsibility for storing it for them. You know we need to have those dormitories ready within two weeks if we are to meet our commitment to students coming in for the third quarter. I know that if we could get some action today from the director of purchasing, the order for the furniture originally requested could be delivered within ten days. Would it be possible for you to go to the state capitol with me and talk to him, and if we can't get any satisfaction from him, perhaps you could talk to Bill Astin, the administrative assistant to the governor, because I am certain that the governor would straighten out his director of purchasing very quickly, particularly in view of some of the newspaper editorials of recent months about the sad state of purchasing within state government."

Parker replied, "I should attend the meeting of the council of presidents, but let me call Bob Jonas, the commissioner of the conference, and see if it is at all possible for me to give him a verbal report which he can then convey to the council of presidents."

Parker's phone rang and his secretary said that Commissioner Jonas was on the line. "Commissioner," Parker began, "I've had an emergency come up here and wonder whether or not any serious harm would be done if I missed the meeting of the presidents scheduled for this afternoon. I can give you a brief summary of the report I would give them, and you can pass it on to them But if you feel that my presence is absolutely essential, I will certainly get away from here some way.

"I would like for you to convey to the presidents that our committee has about four more weeks of investigation, at which time I will make a complete report to them about our athletic problems. Also, please tell them that I am certain everything in the athletic department is now on the up-and-up, since all of their activities are being monitored by my special assistant. Well, what do you think? Is my presence absolutely required, or, no, let's not make it that way . . . do you think that I need to be there today?"

Jonas replied, "No, President Parker, Elgin is not on the agenda today at all. We are simply going to talk about schedules for fall and spring sports next year and some other general matters of business, but we had not planned at all to take up Elgin's case at this meeting."

"Well, convey my regrets, and tell them that I'll see them at the May meeting. And many thanks."

Returning home that evening, Parker was greeted by his wife who said, "The phone has been ringing off the hook. Reporters have been calling you, the three local TV stations have been calling, and I don't know how many radio stations have called."

"What's it all about?" Parker asked.

She replied, "I'm not sure, but I think it has something to do with the athletic program at Elgin and the meeting of the council of presidents of the conference."

Parker went to the phone and called his director of public information, Tim Watts. As soon as Parker identified himself, Watts said, "Boy, am I glad to hear from you, President Parker. Everybody, and I mean everybody, has been calling me. They want to know what our response is to the conference's action of this afternoon."

Parker asked, "What action?"

Tim replied, "They suspended us indefinitely from the conference."

Case Study 7

Dean of Students Bill Morris was in conference with members of his staff discussing the request of the Black United Students organization for a black student center. The formal request for such a center had been made two weeks prior to the opening of school, largely as a result of a series of human relations seminars involving students, faculty, and administrators. Morris was certain that the black students would be satisfied with two or three rooms in the student center and he had assurance from the administration that such space could be made available within two or three months. Though Morris felt he had a good relationship with members of the black student organization, they were becoming increasingly impatient with what they termed the administration's delay in meeting what to them was a reasonable request. In fact, during Morris' last meeting with the president of the Black United Students, the president told him that in his judgment and in the judgment of most of the members of his organization they were experiencing another delaying tactic by the administration designed "to put the darkies in their place."

Morris fully understood the problem faced by the central administration in finding available space in the student center for a black student center; however, he also believed that were such a center to be viewed as a top priority item by the central administration, provision of such space could be expedited. He had called the meeting of his staff to check their reaction to his conclusion, and, assuming they agreed to plan a strategy for bringing some gentle pressure to bear on Dr. Osgood, the university president, to recognize the top priority of the request of the black students.

Morris read to his staff members the letter he had just received from the executive committee of the Black United Students.

Dean Morris,

We do not feel that we can tolerate any longer the unnecessary delay in providing space for black students to meet on this campus, and, more particularly, space that they can call their own. We believe that we have been more patient than the situation would require, and we feel that you and the administration have left us no course other than one which will bring us to a confrontation. As has so often been the case in the past, we find that whenever we discuss an issue, we always come out second best. It seems that we only get something when we confront the administration with demands; then they concede until the pressure is taken off. You will be hearing from us in an appropriate manner soon.

The Black United Student Executive Committee

As Morris finished reading the letter, there was a knock on his door and his secretary entered. She seemed rather upset and walked over to Morris and whispered in his ear, "There are about 150 black students marching toward the administration building, and each of them has a brick in his hand."

Case Study 8

Three instruction (team) leaders in Ellwood School are also very close to the principal. They all teach in quite traditional ways. Angie Brown has student-taught in an "open school" and feels the informal open teaching style is one she strongly supports. Near the end of the school year Angie taught in Ellwood School as a substitute teacher and in the process got to know the teaching staff, including the three instructional leaders. At the end of the year the principal approached Angie and asked her if she would like to teach at Ellwood next year. The principal added, "I would like you to teach on Mrs. Barne's team." (Mrs. Barnes is one of the three traditional team leaders.)

Case Study 9

Mrs. Perkins has been a strong supporter of her daughter's favorite teacher, Sybil Andrews. Shortly after school on Tuesday Mrs. Perkins dropped into Mrs. Andrew's classroom and related the following:

"My daughter just loves your class. It's the only class she talks about at home. Two days ago the school counselor called me in and said that my daughter should seek professional help for her psychological problems. The counselor said that two other teachers—not you—agreed with the recommendation. Your grades and conduct reports have been so supportive! Don't you agree that there is no need for any kind of psychological help?"

Case Study 10

Elliott Jones received this note from the principal's secretary: "Please drop by my office for a chat when you get a chance." Elliott arrived at Principal Ritchie's office within the hour, and Mr. Ritchie said, "I've decided to change the F you gave Buddy Parker in American Government to a D. According to state law he has to have a passing grade in the course in order to graduate, and if he doesn't graduate he can't accept the athletic scholarship he's been offered at the university. Another year of high school wouldn't do Buddy any good anyway. This is a tough decision for me but it had to be made."

Case Study 11

Martha Wright, a first grade teacher at West Ridge, returned to her classroom not sure what, if anything, she could do about an incident that had just occurred in the hallway. She found Robin, a student in Miss Peabody's second grade class, sitting on the hallway floor sobbing, holding a crumpled homework paper in her hand. Martha managed to calm the child and asked her what was the matter. Robin handed Martha the homework paper. The paper was obviously an arithmetic assignment and appeared to be correct in every detail. At the bottom of the page in a second grader's printing style were the words, "I love you Miss Peabody." In red pencil followed the statement, "Keep your mind on your work!"

The incident with Robin was not the first reason Martha had had for concern about Miss Peabody's style of working with children. Several of her students from last year had come to her with accounts of Miss Peabody's tactics for maintaining discipline. Standing in the corner with a book balanced on the head, being called to the front of the room and having to write how "bad" one was or how "stupid," having to write five hundred "I will never's," all were apparently frequent occurrences in Miss Peabody's room.

Martha, after hearing these accounts from her former students, had chatted informally about them with Miss Peabody in the teachers lounge. Miss Peabody's notion was that students in the second grade needed to be disciplined if they were to be managed at all. As she put it, "The typical seven- or eight-year-old will take over the classroom unless the authority of the teacher is established early and firmly." Martha had not raised the question again though she had frequently met Miss Peabody in the teachers lounge and talked to her about school matters in general.

Martha wondered about her responsibilities as a teacher. She was certain that Miss Peabody was teaching in a manner that was likely to harm several children, possibly some of them seriously. Should she talk to Miss Peabody again? Should she share her concern with some other teachers? talk to the principal about it? forget it? or what?

Case Study 12

Frank Walton had been principal at Perkins Elementary School for the past month. It was his first principalship, and he felt quite fortunate to have the opportunity to gain his initial administrative experience in a school system where principals were granted considerable autonomy in working with their faculty to plan and carry out innovative curriculum and instructional programs. He felt assured of support from the central office, particularly from the superintendent who had told him when he assumed his position, "Now, Frank, this is your school, and I expect you to run it. If you need help, call me. Otherwise, identify and solve your own problems."

Frank also had every reason to be pleased with his teaching staff. They were an energetic group, and dedicated to making their school the best one in the country. Frank found that they shared experiences, offered constructive criticism to each other, and volunteered to assist each other with special projects, often teaming to carry out some lesson plans, and even changing classes from time to time.

Frank had encountered one problem that concerned him, and he had not yet determined just how to solve it, or even if it could be solved. It involved Miss Jones, who was the elementary curriculum supervisor for the school system. Miss Jones had been in the system some thirty-five years, twenty of which she had served as supervisor. She came to the school at least once a month and after stopping by Frank's office to bring him greetings from the central office, she would visit the classrooms in the school and offer suggestions to the teachers, not all of which they particularly welcomed. Frank had twice mentioned to Miss Jones that it might be better if she visited only those classrooms to which she was invited by the teacher. Miss Jones replied that she felt it was her responsibility to visit each classroom to make sure that the quality of instruction in the school measured up to the standards expected in the county. Miss Jones was now visiting some of the classrooms, and Frank hoped that she would not upset any of his teachers.

There was a knock at the door, and Frank said, "Come in." Mrs. Walton, a fourth grade teacher in the school, entered. She was obviously upset, and as she spoke she began to cry.

"You'll have to get Miss Jones out of my classroom. I can't stand it another minute. She's embarrassed me now for the last time. I was teaching a lesson in arithmetic and she stood up right in the middle of one of my sentences and said, 'Let me show you how to do that, Miss Walton. I can see that you must not have thought this lesson through properly. Here, I'll take over. Now you just sit down and watch.' "

Frank said, "Now, calm down, Alice, and let's talk about it. Is she in the classroom now teaching class?"

Miss Walton replied, "Yes, she is, and as far as I'm concerned she's disruptive every time she appears. I don't like to give ultimatums, but if she walks into my classroom again I'm walking out, and I don't intend to return. I believe I know how to do my job, and I think I do it rather well. I would hope that you as principal would help me continue to do that job well. One way you can help, and I suppose the most help you can really give me, is to keep Miss Jones out of my classroom."

Case Study 13

"Jerry and Bill took acid on our field trip yesterday, Miss Parks," said Sandra as she and her girl friend stood in front of Miss Parks' desk. "How do you know that?" responded Miss Parks who wasn't aware of much of anything about the field trip since there was so much noise and confusion. "I saw them take it in sugar cubes," answered Sandra's friend. "They took it on the bus!"

Miss Parks asked the two girls what they thought should be done about the matter. "We want you to go to the principal with us," replied the girls. Once in the principal's office the girls retold the story. The principal's first question was, "How many students know about this?" "Oh, Jerry and Bill were bragging about it to everyone on the bus! The whole school knows by now," responded the girls. The principal thanked the girls and said that he would take care of the matter.

The next day the principal called the field trip sponsors and the teachers of Jerry and Bill into his office. "I think I'm going to expel Jerry and Bill for the remaining two weeks of school this year," said the principal. "I don't know for sure if they took LSD or just plain sugar cubes but if we let them get away with their bragging we'll just make heroes out of them. I want to nip this drug problem in the bud. Miss Parks, you were the main class sponsor on the field trip. What do you think?"

Notes for Chapter 6

1. See the value hierarchy in the introduction to Part 2.

2. Some will argue that the aggressor might be disuaded or that one should shoot to wound rather than to kill. The immediacy of the forced-choice situation does not give the subject the benefit of being "Monday morning quarterback." A man makes his decision on the basis of what seems reasonable at the time and the courts judge him accordingly.

(7)

Category Three: A Constellation of Values

These operational guides focus on your values, with particular emphasis on the fact that these values constantly change. They change as you encounter new situations, meet new people, and face new decisions.

We emphasize that you should be alert to the fact that your values do change and that that change is reflected in the decisions you make. We would ask that you recognize that what you do reflects more accurately what your values are than does what you say they are. As a colleague said, "I do not care to hear so much about what you say you believe. I prefer to watch you act and then ask you what you took for granted when you took that action."

It will be interesting to compare your application of a particular guide to a case to see whether or not it is the same application or follows the same guide as applied by someone else. You might find that in certain situations your value hierarchy differs so dramatically from someone else's that they are viewing the situation as a choice from among several "bad" alternatives while you are viewing it as a choice from among several "good" alternatives.

Operational Guide 6

Actions of a decision-maker should support what he states as his real goals and/or objectives.

What this guide means is that the teacher should take his or her objectives seriously. It is very easy for a person in an organization to become a victim of goal displacement, meaning that the decision-maker focuses on objectives to the extent that they become goals. Teacher A, for example, wants to teach a particular thing but a boy who is snapping gum annoys her so that she no longer pursues her original goal.

Subject matter in schools is both an end and a means—an end in schools as presently structured and a means in terms of student learning except to produce incipient scholars. The norms of the school require students to memorize and do busy work with subject matter so that they can be rewarded with the currency of the school, good grades. In this sense, subject matter is an end in itself. At the same time, those educators who take other goals seriously—e.g., self-actualization—see subject matter as a means for reaching other more important goals.

Function five, providing the conditions for personal or self-development, is largely achieved through idiosyncratic behavior of teachers. This is especially true in curriculum and instruction as contrasted with extracurriculur activities, for there is rarely much of a support system in curriculum and instruction in behalf of goals such as self-actualization. This is to say that teachers are seldom rewarded by the administration for meeting the immediate needs of the individual students. One reason for this is the difficulty in quantifying student progress toward such goals. It takes a secure teacher to deviate from the main goal—the production of incipient scholars—and the uncertain teacher will probably revert to the status quo. The following account by a second year teacher demonstrates what happens all too often:

> Last summer I had an excellent course titled Humanistic Education. We talked about the emotional needs of children and how schools emphasize thinking at the expense of feeling. I was really turned on by the ideas and developed a number of lesson plans to try out in the fall. When I started teaching in the fall, I used some of the ideas but found out that they didn't fit into my teaching schedule. The schedule always gave me security and when one of the new ideas I learned last summer lasted too long or worse yet just didn't work my

whole schedule for the day was messed up. Besides that, I had to adjust to the school's schedule for recess, lunch, music, etc.

Operational Guide 7

Be aware that your own values should change as different situations present themselves.

We are constantly reminded in the literature on the present era that change is the only absolute. Technological advancements add to the psychological climate of change, and man's nervous system must adjust so that he can relearn his environment from moment to moment.[1] To fail to do so is to flirt with the kind of extinction whereby one is no longer taken seriously by those who can make such adjustments. At the same time, the decision-maker needs to establish stability zones that give him confidence in his decision-making. (Note that we said *zones* rather than absolute ideas.) Such zones give him an opportunity to reflect on the matter of who he is, what he believes in, and what he intends to do about his beliefs.

Educational decision-maker Smith teaches in a large urban school where change has been especially acute. She has experienced four different principals in five years, the change of the population of her school from primarily white to 60 percent black and 40 percent white as a result of busing, and the influx of a multitude of new teaching materials and methods. Amidst such changes the teacher has certain stability zones that help her stay on top of any situation. She enjoys inservice courses, for example, and she enjoys reading. She does not view any particular course as the answer to all situations nor does she rely on any particular book or journal as her "bible."[2] She has both flexibility and confidence.

The challenge to the educational decision-maker is to find ways in which he can assess both his own values and the organization's values at any given time, for the educator is so involved in the moment-to-moment and day-to-day decisions that he may fail to know when his own values and the organization's values have changed. The teacher who operates under the adage that "when the door closes the students are mine" often confuses independence with expertise. In fact, her expertise as an educational decision-maker depends on her ability to acquire information as to her own value system and that of the environment in which she should operate. (Many teachers try to limit that environment to the classroom, but, as we have pointed out, this is impossible given authority and influence directed at all members of the school as a social system.) The question then becomes, "How can

I as an educational decision-maker acquire information about myself and the environment in which I operate in order to deal effectively with the changes that occur, or should occur, both in myself and the environment?

In chapter 1 we discussed indicators in the school, the school district, the community, and residential areas that can give us information as to the norms of the school as a social system. In chapters 2 and 3 we discussed purposes and functions of the school with an eye on the acquisition of information as to school norms. Finally, in the introduction to the present section, Part II, we focused on value hierarchies of individual decision-makers. We hope that in our discussion of these matters you have seen that confident flexibility on the part of the decision-maker is more a matter of attitude than of formula or recipe. It is part of the process that we have identified as self-actualization, for no person can prescribe in a particular situation precisely what you should do in order to be an effective educational decision-maker.

A first grade teacher worked out her own system for determining whether or not her value hierarchy was being implemented. This hierarchy took the form of three major questions:

(1) Does the child want to return to school on Monday?

(2) Do my teaching and the school environment encourage and broaden the child's innate curiosity?

(3) Does the child with my help and the aid of the school environment develop the skills and ability to satisfy that curiosity?

An eighth grade teacher had certain checkpoints in mind that helped him assess whether or not his value hierarchy was being implemented. He expected his students to:

(1) Engage themselves in a variety of activities and projects in his classroom and the school as a whole;

(2) Cooperate with each other on such activities and projects and in the process teach each other and learn from each other;

(3) Tell him in a number of verbal and nonverbal ways that they enjoyed being in school.

An eleventh grade American history teacher had a different set of indicators in the form of questions:

(1) Has the material been covered—that is, will the students get through with the part of the text that covers the Civil War (1861–1865) by Christmas and the part of the text that discusses the war in Indochina by the end of the school year?

(2) Have the students demonstrated that they have learned the most important facts about the eras covered in the textbook?

(3) Have the students, at least a few who are good students, enjoyed the material read and the type of examinations given knowing that such an approach will help them prepare for similar approaches when they get to college?

(4) Will the students, especially the good students, recognize that I am a scholar—the kind of scholar who could well teach at the university level some day?

We can see from these three teachers' goals that there are differences among teachers as to what they value most. What is important for all teachers and administrators, regardless of their value hierarchies, is that they have discovered and used a variety of techniques to reflect on: (1) whether or not they are making educational decisions consistent with their value hierarchy; (2) the relationship between their own personal belief system and the norms of the school; and (3) ways in which their own and the school system's values can be flexible and still assure them the confidence they need as educational decision-makers.

One of the most useful approaches to reflecting on belief systems is included in the conclusion to the introduction to Part 2. The decision-maker is asked to build a case for the antithesis of his basic assumptions. He is then asked to project such assumptions into the areas of curriculum and instruction so that implications of assumptions can be examined. For example, the eleventh grade American history teacher's pattern for reflection might look like the following:

Pluses	*Minuses*
Students should cover the first half of the book by the Christmas break and the entire book by the end of the year.	Students should not cover the first half of the book by the Christmas break and the entire book by the end of the year.
Students should demonstrate that they have learned the most important facts in the textbook.	Students shouldn't demonstrate that they have learned the most important facts in the textbook.
Students, at least a few who are good students, should enjoy the material read and the type of examinations given knowing that such an approach will help them prepare for similar approaches when they get to college.	Students, at least a few who are good students, shouldn't enjoy the material read and the type of examinations given knowing that such an approach will help them prepare for similar approaches when they get to college.
Students, especially the good students, should recognize that I am a scholar—the kind of scholar who could well teach at the university level some day.	Students, especially the good students, shouldn't recognize that I am a scholar—the kind of scholar who could well teach at the university level some day.

We will now take item four and build a case for the antithesis of the eleventh grade history teacher's basic assumption.

> Why should students, especially the good students, have to recognize that I am a scholar—the kind that could well teach at the university level some day? It's simply an ego trip for me to lay this on the students. Anyway, I may well be treating my eleventh graders as college students simply because I would rather be teaching at the university level. Eleventh graders have their own needs for this time of their development and I may be pushing my belief in scholarship on them at a time when they have more important needs.

What we are suggesting is that the educational decision-maker be the kind of reflective thinker who bounces ideas back and forth so that he cannot only revise his own value system for a given situation but can also better understand the value systems of those he encounters in such situations.

Operational Guide 8

As all decisions affecting groups focus on the relationship between freedom and order, the more order the less individual freedom, and conversely.

This postulate is truly a dilemma of group behavior. The decision-maker must realize that every decision limits options and the likelihood that chance will be effectively reckoned with. In trying to define the parameters of acceptable group behavior, the decision-maker limits the options of others.

It is part of the myth surrounding teaching and teachers that the good teacher is the teacher who makes a large number of decisions affecting the entire group of students with whom she works. Contrary to popular belief, the good teacher may well be the teacher who makes the fewest decisions affecting the whole group. The teacher who is highly organized and has detailed lesson plans may well be limiting the freedom of her students so that less valuable learning takes place.[3] In effect, what the teacher as educational decision-maker needs to do is to strike a balance between random, often unconscious teaching and highly rigid teaching. John A. Zahorik, who has done considerable research in this field of study, suggests this compromise: "Those teacher actions that are not greatly influenced by student reactions or other classroom events can be planned specifically, while those that are influenced by what happens during the course of a lesson can be planned less specifically."[4]

A great deal of attention is given in educational rhetoric to individualizing instruction so that student needs can be met. It is a truism that learning is highly individual and hence often takes place in the form of what an observer might judge to be random behavior, although such behavior is not really random from the learner's point of view. As educational planners we are faced with the paradox of providing for random and highly individualized behavior by systematic instruction.

The issue is somewhat clouded by the way the teacher identifies and relates to the "deviant" child. According to some teachers the way to control the behavior of the "deviant" is to control the behavior of all involved. This is to say that what's good for some is good for all. Such a view is certainly consistent with the bureaucratic model: "The majority of the good people have to pay for the mistakes of the few bad people." However, the way to ensure the freedom to create, innovate, and develop as an individual is to grant freedom to all. We are faced with the dilemma that focuses on the relationship between freedom and authority, freedom and responsibility, external control and creativity.

Case Study 1

Martin James was an instructor in the accounting department of the School of Business. He was also mayor of a small town, a suburb of the large city in which the university was located. James was an influential figure in the state Democratic Party, having served two terms on that party's state committee. He had been active in the current gubernatorial campaign, though his political activities had not ostensibly interfered with the performance of his instructional duties.

James was beginning his third year at the university, and as with all untenured faculty on one-year contracts he was considered by a promotions committee composed of senior faculty and the dean from the School of Business for reemployment as an instructor for another year, or for promotion to assistant professor, or for discontinuation of his contract. The committee recommended to the president of the university that James's contract not be renewed and that James be notified within thirty days that his services would be required only until the end of the current academic year.

President Watson reviewed the minutes of the promotions committee. It seemed obvious to him that James had generated more than the normal amount of complaints from his students; specifically, the students had complained on numerous occasions that he was late to class or did not meet class, that he constantly badgered students, and that his knowledge of his subject, or at least his presentation of that knowledge, left much to be desired. Three colleagues in the Department of Accounting had registered formal complaints with the dean about James's teaching. Based on this evidence, President Watson told the dean of the School of Business to proceed with the formalities of notifying James of the decisions regarding his continued employment and of his right of formal appeal. The dean talked with James and reported to the president that James seemed to understand and accept the decision. He made no request for an appeal of the decision not to renew his contract.

Two days later, President Watson received a call from the lieutenant governor who asked about the case of Mr. James and indicated that he was concerned that the Democratic Party might cite James's case as an example of political influence in higher education. (The lieutenant governor, a Republican, was his party's candidate for governor.) He asked President Watson if he would review James's case to make certain that there was no political influence. Watson agreed to do so.

A day later, the speaker of the house, a Democrat, called President Watson and indicated grave concern over the political influence being exercised within the university as exemplified by the discharge of Mr. James. He said that he intended to investigate the matter unless he could be fully satisfied that politics had not been involved in the decision to dismiss Mr. James. He suggested that everyone would be saved much trouble if Mr. James were reemployed for the following year, and asked that President Watson give that alternative serious consideration. He then thanked Watson for his courtesy and indicated that he would like to hear from him within the week.

Case Study 2

John McIntosh assumed the presidency of Urban University three months before the date set for review of the university's budget by the governor's Advisory Budget Commission. McIntosh and his staff had carefully prepared a budget that reflected the dramatic needs of Urban University due to its rapid growth, combined with years of modest appropriations from the legislation. Though Urban University was now the third largest university in the state, its total appropriations from the state placed it twelfth among the fourteen state universities. In per-pupil dollar allocations, it was the lowest in the state and had been since becoming a part of the state university system.

After careful study, McIntosh and his staff had concluded that for the university to receive appropriations parity with the two other universities similar to it in size and programs, a 230 percent increase in its operational budget would be required. Though some of the funds could be generated from increased student fees, grants, and tuition increases, McIntosh and his staff concluded that the university should request an increase of 189 percent in state appropriations to Urban University.

On the day that Urban University was to present its case to the governor's Advisory Budget Commission, McIntosh and the chairman of his Board of Trustees met for an early breakfast and discussed in detail the presentation to be made. The chairman of the board, though fully supporting the budget request—as had the full board—expressed some trepidation about the response the governor and the members of the commission might make. As he put it, "Though our request is reasonable from our point of view, I fear that it may not be reasonable from the point of view of the commission. Do you think we should be prepared to hedge quite a bit?"

McIntosh replied, "I don't think so. I believe that our request is a fair one and is really designed to make up for many years of neglect. If the money is not available, that is one thing, but at least we will have gone on record as justifying the increase we asked for." At the end of breakfast the board chairman agreed with McIntosh's conclusion, and they left for the state capitol and the budget hearings.

The budget hearing began at 9:30 a.m., and by 11:15 McIntosh had concluded his presentation. All members of the budget commission had been supplied in advance with a concise summary of the budget request, and McIntosh supplemented that information by discussing the budget request and showing supporting documents, many of which were presented graphically through the use of charts and other visual aids. At the end of McIntosh's presentation, the governor looked up from the last page of the budgetary request and asked, "President McIntosh, do you truly believe that this is a realistic request to place before this commission?"

Case Study 3

Dean Jarrett was charged by the faculty of the College of Arts and Sciences with policing student admission to the college. During the past three years the Central Admissions Office had admitted students to the College of Arts and Sciences who did not meet the standards prescribed by the faculty of that college. Recently Jarrett had several conversations with the university dean of admissions and was assured by him that the standards established by the faculty were the standards that the Central Admissions Office applied when it admitted students. Jarrett had requested and received all the admissions folders of students admitted for the coming year, and all did meet the standards as set forth by the faculty of the college. On the opening day of orientation, however, there were fifteen students for whom Jarrett had no folders. All fifteen were male and exceedingly healthy, ranging in height from six feet to six feet nine inches and in weight from about 190 to 270 pounds. After the orientation meeting Jarrett called the dean of admissions and asked about the folders on the fifteen students. He was told that information was still being gathered for those folders and would be available by the following Monday.

On Monday, Jarrett visited the dean of admissions and looked at the folders on the fifteen students. None met the standards as established by the faculty. When questioned about this fact, the dean of admissions said, "These men are special admissions cases directed to be admitted to the university by the president. I have no control over their admissions since the president personally requested that they be admitted." Jarrett replied, "But you realize that under the admissions policy adopted by the Board of Trustees the faculty of each school is responsible for setting the admissions requirements for that school." The dean of admissions replied, "Yes, I am fully aware of that policy, but I repeat, I was directed by the president of the university to admit these fifteen students. If you have any question about their admission, I would suggest you see the president and discuss the policy and his action with him."

Returning to his office after the conversation with the dean of admissions, Jarrett received a call from the dean of arts and sciences. During the call the dean requested that Jarrett prepare for the faculty meeting two weeks hence a report to the faculty on student admissions, and that Jarrett give particular attention to the faculty's concern over the application of the admissions standards it had approved.

Case Study 4

Tom White had been chairman of the Department of Education at the university for three months. When he was offered the position he was assured by the dean of the College of Arts and Sciences, his immediate superior, that the university wanted to make major strides in developing programs in professional education that would serve as a model for the entire southeastern region of the United States. Another major reason White accepted the job was that a private foundation had recently granted the university $3,500,000 to develop a program in preschool education. Funding for the program had been provided for five years with a reasonable assurance that it would be again funded if it were successful. This project, entitled "The Instructional Development Project," was to involve the Department of Education, other social science departments in the College of Arts and Sciences, and the public schools of surrounding counties. White had assumed that the Department of Education would play a major role in planning and developing the project, but within a month after becoming chairman he knew that assumption to be invalid.

The project operated out of the office of Mark Capps, vice-president for Planning and Development and a part-time member of the Department of Education, who taught no classes. Bob Smart, the director of the project holding an adjunct professorship in the Department of Education, reported to a policy board composed of the vice-president for Planning and Development as chairman, the superintendents of the local public schools, and the chairmen of the departments of psychology and education. At the second meeting of the board attended by White he raised the question of the relationship between the project and the Department of Education. He stated that it seemed to him that many efforts were being duplicated in that the project was employing people with the same expertise already present in the Department of Education. He also said that relations with the local school units were not coordinated between the Department of Education and the Instructional Development Project.

The chairman of the board responded that the Instructional Development Project was an all-university responsibility and was not to be viewed as having any greater relationship to the Department of Education than it had to the other participating department, Social Science. White then pointed out that school people with whom the project was working and for whom it was developing programs looked to the Department of Education as the unit within the university primarily responsible for maintaining liaison between school systems and the university. The meeting ended with a suggestion from the board chairman that the director of the project and White get together and discuss mutual objectives and ways that such objectives might be achieved.

The following day, White and the director of the project had lunch and discussed their perceptions of the educational development project in terms of its purposes and organizational responsibilities. The project director made it clear that he had been brought to the university with the understanding that he was to report to the vice-president for Planning and Development and to his board of directors as he carried out his responsibility of developing innovative programs for the public schools. He added that he felt no direct responsibility to the Department of Education, and in his judgment there were few people in the department who could contribute positively to the development of the programs he wished to develop. Near the end of the conversation he stated, "Had the Department of Education been capable of carrying out such a program, I doubt very much that I would have been asked to come to the university. It is my understanding that the granting agency provided funds for this project with the condition that the Department of Education not be primarily responsible for it."

Returning to his office, White found three members of his department waiting for him. He invited them into the office, and once all were seated Professor Smith, the senior member, began, "The three of us are very concerned about events in the Instructional Development Project. As you know, our field is early childhood education, and we have been working for several years with the local public school systems in generating programs to upgrade their efforts in early childhood education. For the last several weeks we have received several calls from elementary principals, and from one associate superintendent for elementary education, expressing concern about their relationships with people in the Instructional Development Project. They feel that most people they come into contact with from the project usually let it be known that they have a very low opinion of the current efforts of the public school systems and the

Department of Education. They point out that project personnel want to try out programs in the public schools, but do not feel that public school personnel should interfere to the point of vetoing development projects proposed by personnel of the Instructional Development Project. We think, Tom, that something will have to be done soon to clarify just what relationship should exist between the Department of Education and the Instructional Development Project."

White thanked the professors and assured them that he would think carefully about the issue they had raised. He saw them to the door and as he returned to his desk his secretary told him that Vice-President Capps was on the phone. Capps asked how the conversation had gone between White and the director of the Instructional Development Project. White replied that it was a candid conversation and that although there were differences they probably could be worked out. Capps then asked, "What do you think about adjunct appointments for three people that Bob wants to bring into the Instructional Development Project? They are top flight people, but I know that we can't get them unless we also give them faculty appointments. Obviously, we would want you to look at their credentials and approve them based on the quality of their credentials, but I think it essential to the project that we bring in these three people, and I am sure they are ready to come if you can offer them appointments in the Department of Education."

White said, "Well, Mark, you realize I'll have to consult with the members of the department about such appointments, but I think there are several other issues that need to be decided before we deal with adjunct appointments in the Department of Education for staff brought here to work full time in the educational improvement project."

Capps replied, "I am sure that there are other things we need to discuss, but it's important that we make a concrete offer to these people within two or three weeks, or we just might lose them. So I'd like you to deal with that issue now, and we'll talk about the others later on. I'll get back to you in about a week to find out how we need to proceed. Let me know if you have any questions."

White's secretary came in and placed on his desk a brown manila envelope. He opened it and took out copies of three vitae and a note from Bob Smart. The note read: "Here are vitae on the three men I am hoping to bring to the campus next week. We have made them tentative offers, but I am sure they will not accept them unless they receive adjunct appointments in the Department of Education. I am sure you will want to cooperate fully in this matter. Many thanks. Sincerely, Bob."

Case Study 5

In September the Caldwell School Board voted 5-3 not to renew Superintendent Williams' contract. The chairwoman of the board led the fight against Superintendent Williams, saying, "Sure, Mr. Williams has built new facilities here and has passed bond issues, but he just doesn't have good public relations with people in the community. He hasn't shown me the proper consideration as board chairwoman from the start." Superintendent Williams' reaction to the board decision was clear and consistent: "I've spent a great deal of time and energy in bringing this school system to the position we've achieved. We have two new elementary schools and a new high school with a modern auditorium, a half-million dollar football stadium, and a fifty-thousand dollar baseball field. The community's support is evident in their passing of bond issues. Although I will have to seek new employment, my main interest right now is in providing the best education for our students during the current school year."

Within the next two months two board members, including the chairwoman, resigned. Her husband had been transferred to another state. The other member resigned for business reasons. Two black members of the community were elected, largely through concentrated efforts by leadership within the black community. (Blacks constituted nearly 50 percent of the community of Caldwell.)

One of the first things the new board did was to vote by a 4-3 margin to give Superintendent Williams a new two-year contract, in spite of the fact that the new chairwoman of the board also opposed Superintendent Williams. (One of the board members did not vote; he was out of town.)

On a Monday morning in November one of the newly elected board members arrived in Jo Bardolf's classroom half an hour before school started. He introduced himself and then said, "You know that my election was a result of the community's desire to know about and improve our schools. What do you think about Superintendent Williams' leadership? What are some of the problems you face as a teacher in our community?"

Case Study 6

Mat Johnson, dean of the School of Business, picked up the phone and listened as a man who identified himself as Detective Sergeant Miller said, "Dean Johnson, if you can get down here in the next hour, I think it would be in your best interest to do so." Johnson responded, "What's this all about? What do you mean 'get down in the next hour'? I am rather busy and I don't know whether I can make it or not. Can't you tell me more?" The sergeant replied, "I can't tell you anything else except to say that I think it would be best for you to come down right away. I'll meet you at the 15th Street entrance, if you think you can get here within thirty minutes. Otherwise, come to my office at 304 Municipal Building. I am sorry that I can't tell you anything else, but again let me say that I believe you should come down right away." Johnson answered, "All right, this is certainly strange, but you've convinced me. I'm on my way."

At the entrance to the municipal building Johnson was met by the detective sergeant and together they proceeded to a third floor room. Entering the room Johnson saw the chairman of his Business Management Department, Bill Malvren, seated in a straight-backed wooden chair, facing two officers. One of the officers was speaking.

"Dr. Malvren, you realize that this statement you are about to sign may be used against you in a court of law. You understand that you may have an attorney present, and that an attorney may advise you not to sign this statement. Are you sure that you want to sign it?"

Bill Malvren answered, "Yes, I am sure that I want to sign it and I do understand that my attorney can be present, but I just want to sign it and get it over with."

"Don't sign anything, Bill, until we have had a chance to talk, and you should consult an attorney," said Johnson. "I don't know what this is all about, but I don't want you to sign a statement in police headquarters without some legal advice." He walked over to Malvren and asked, "What's this all about, Bill?" Malvren took the statement from the officer and handed it to Johnson. Johnson read: "I, William Malvren, admit that on the 15th of February at approximately 2:00 p.m. in the men's room of the 10th Street Library I did solicit for the purpose of committing a homosexual act a certain man, then unknown to me, but now known to me to be Detective

W. H. Watson. I have made this statement willingly with the foreknowledge that it may be used against me in a court of law. To the best of my knowledge all the foregoing statements are true. Signed, William Malvren."

Johnson turned to the detective sergeant. "How long do you plan to hold him?" The sergeant replied, "We can release him now in your custody if you will guarantee that he will not leave the city within the next week." Johnson said that he could "guarantee that" and, turning to Malvren, said, "Come on, Bill, let me take you home."

During the ride home Malvren said at least four or five times how sorry he was to put Johnson in such an embarrassing position, but that he just hadn't known where to turn. Johnson told him not to feel that he had to talk now: he could come to Johnson's office in the morning and discuss the whole matter and what might be done.

Driving back to his office Johnson reflected on his twelve-year association with Bill Malvren. Both the Johnson and Malvren children had been close and had frequently visited with each other. Bill's wife Sue was a teacher in the elementary school that Johnson's youngest child attended, and had taught one of the older Johnson children. Malvren had been an able teacher and chairman, and, to the best of Johnson's knowledge, an exemplary husband and father.

Arriving at his office Johnson pulled from his in-basket a memorandum that had come from the president the day before. The memorandum read:

Confidential to All Deans

Subject: Recent Board Discussion of Problems of Homosexuality on Campus

1. The Board spent more than 1½ hours at its last meeting discussing recent problems with homosexuality on campus. Much to my chagrin, the discussion became much more emotional than I think it should have been. Despite the lack of concrete evidence, and in the face of changing times, many of our board members seem convinced that we have a serious problem here. In my opinion, the matter is not truly serious, but if many of the board members percieve it to be so then I suppose we have to accept that at least their perceptions are a problem to us.

2. The purpose of this memo is simply to alert you to the board's concern and also to request that any incidents which you feel might reinforce this concern be brought immediately to my attention.

Case Study 7

Jack Watson had been director of development at the university for the past three years. He had had some fifteen years experience in development work at two other universities, but this was his first opportunity to head the development office. Soon after he began work he had recommended to the president that a major fund drive be undertaken to raise money for scholarships, supplemental salaries for faculty, and supplemental funds for research projects. Watson's proposal was enthusiastically endorsed by the president, his staff, and the faculty, and the campaign began in Watson's second year.

The first year of the campaign was quite successful, resulting in more than $110,000 from alumni and friends and staff of the university. The goal for the current year was $300,000, and as the campaign began Watson had every reason to believe that it would meet with success. But several events had occurred soon after school began. Some controversial speakers had been brought to campus, raising the ire of some of the local citizens who had been major contributors. A group of students and faculty regularly attended city council meetings and took every opportunity to protest the current attitude of the city fathers toward welfare and race relations. And finally, the Student Life Policies Committee had just approved for campus recognition the Students for a Democratic Society, which had created quite a stir among some of the alumni and other supporters of the university throughout the state.

Watson looked at the memo he had just received from President Morgan:

To: Tom Watson
From: President Morgan
Subject: Current Commitment Campaign

I have been receiving communications such as the attached from several sources, and I wonder how seriously such communications, and particularly the attitudes they reflect, will affect our fund raising campaign this year.

As you know, we have budgeted $300,000 income from the campaign. Though we could do without some of those funds, it would be most embarrassing for us not to achieve the goal this year, particularly in light of the success we met this past year.

Would you at your earliest convenience give me your assessment of the current situation and any recommendations for dealing effectively with the negative sentiment about the University expressed at this time by many of our strongest supporters.

Watson glanced at the letter attached to the memo, and saw that it was signed by a major contributor to the Commitment Fund and one who had served as chairman of the Industrial Gifts Committee, a committee that had raised some $40,000 the previous year.

Dear President Morgan:

This brief note is to acquaint you with the formation of the Concerned Citizen's Council, whose express purpose it is to withhold and divert funds from the Committee to the University Drive which you are conducting, as long as subversive elements—and speakers—are being subsidized with the taxpayer's money.

As a state supported institution, the University cannot thumb its nose at the citizens of the state. While we do not wish to control the University, we do feel as taxpayers and parents that we have a right to be heard. In spite of what the students believe, the school does not receive its money from Santa Claus or Chairman Mao! We plan to strike where it hurts the most: the pocketbook. We will operate among businessmen, citizen's groups, legislators, and alumni.

In view of recent reports by the F.B.I. which reveal that the S.D.S. contains subversive elements whose intent it is to overthrow the government of the United States, we cannot buy your naive view that this is "just another student group." We suggest that you read the charter. As President of the University, you will either have to control those fifteen students for whom you have alienated a substantial part of the citizenry of the Huntington area, or we will have your hide!

John J. Sarazen
Concerned Citizen's Council

cc: Governor A. H. Manly
Senator J. D. Marsh

Case Study 8

Janet Sprindle, a first year teacher at Jefferson High School, was trying to determine what her principal was all about. In one teachers' meeting Jones, the principal, asked two coaches to take the school's camera on top of the gym roof to take pictures of smokers behind the gym. "Parents demand evidence for expulsion these days," he said. On another occasion Miss Sprindle's class was interrupted by a public address announcement: "Anyone caught in the tunnels under the school will be suspended." While walking through the boiler room one day, the principal saw a manhole cover on the floor jiggle, and then a boy and a girl emerged. On a third occasion the principal was hung in effigy by the students, after which he took the dummy and placed it in the chair behind his desk.

During the school year Janet tried to teach her students the importance of cooperation. As an example of a fiercely competitive point of view she quoted a Russian expression, *Kto kovo,* which means Who gets whom, or Dog eat dog! Janet concluded by saying that there is much more to life than this.

Shortly after presenting her views on the importance of cooperation, Janet attended the senior banquet along with the seniors in her classes. The principal's speech was on "Locker Room Slogans and Their Meaning in Life." Beginning with "A winner never quits and a quitter never wins," the principal went through a series of slogans that centered on the desirability of stiff competition. He finished his speech by saying, "Life after graduation is 'dog eat dog' and you have to be prepared for this!"

During Janet's first hour American Government class she was asked what she thought about her principal's speech the night before.

Case Study 9

Jack Williams is a teacher in the Ellwood Elementary School. Much to his satisfaction, the assistant superintendent told him that he was being seriously considered for a principalship the following fall. The only opposition voiced to the superintendent was from Jack's principal at Ellwood. She said that "Jack's teaching is often more liberal than I like." Jack is on a school curriculum committee chaired by the Ellwood principal. Two members of the committee share Jack's liberal persuasion whereas two others are close to the principal's more traditional views. Jack contemplates his involvement on the curriculum committee.

Case Study 10

The teachers' lounge at Ellwood School was the center for much gossip, discussion, and heated argument. Tuesday morning was no exception as Tom Jackson, the assistant principal, began his daily sermon.

"What's wrong with schools today is that students are polarized.

Eighty percent of them are O K but you simply can't reach the other 20 percent. And I can tell you who's in that 20 percent—the ones who simply won't respond to anything. They're usually listless, sometimes because they're zonked on drugs. Then there's the second group—the spoiled brats. Another group would always rather be doing something else. But the worst of the 20 percent are the black militants because you can't reach them as individuals. They're always hiding behind their group or ideology."

Loretta, who had nodded her head during much of Tom's speech, now openly supported Tom's views. "I agree with what you're saying about polarization. Another example is that the blacks in the school stay together and so do the whites. But I think the 80 percent who are O K can be divided into groups too. About 20 percent take care of themselves and get good grades even when they don't especially like the courses, but about 60 percent of the 80 percent are interested in some subjects and not in others and they won't just grind it out in order to get good grades. These are the ones you have to teach to in order to win them over to subjects you're interested in."

Dick Richardson, whose idealism was always apparent, was really excited by Tom's and Loretta's comments. "I think you're both wrong—very, very wrong. You can reach all of the students if you simply know how to tap their interests. A good example of that is a student I had last year. He did poorly in all subjects except art. I let him work on his drawing in my class and we started communicating."

"He still can't read or write though," Loretta added. "You didn't really help him at all!"

"At least he enjoyed one class a day and didn't think school was all bad," Dick retorted. "His children may not get a completely one-sided negative view of school when he's a parent."

At this point the principal walked in and was given a brief summary of the discussion. "I know what you're saying about how some students just shouldn't be here. In fact, some of the 20 percent are really dangerous and we're lucky if no one gets hurt during the year. But I think you have to be much more tolerant as a teacher the lower the grade level. In elementary school you should treat all children as if they can be reached. In the latter part of the junior high school you can just write some students off and wait for them to drop out.

If they stay on for high school you should tolerate them only so far and then expel them if they get out of line. They're at the school-leaving age anyway."

Throughout the heated discussion Jan Prickett and Jim Hoenig, both second year teachers, said nothing. The principal now turned to them and said, "What do you think of all this, Jan and Jim?"

Notes for Chapter 7

1. Alvin Toffler, *Future Shock* (New York: Bantam Books, 1971), p. 180.

2. To do so would be folly in light of the fact that it is estimated that the amount of information available to the literate world doubles every fifteen years or so and the number of book titles printed mushroomed from ten thousand in 1960 to seventy thousand in 1970. For a discussion of this matter, see J. C. R. Licklider, *Libraries of the Future* (Cambridge: Massachusetts Institute of Technology Press, 1965), p. 15, and Toffler, *Future Shock*, pp. 152-181.

3. Support for this view is found in the research of John A. Zahorik, professor of education at the University of Wisconsin, Milwaukee. "The Effect of Planning on Teaching," *Elementary School Journal* 71 (December 1970): 143-151.

4. John A. Zahorik and Dale L. Brubaker, *Decisions in Planning for Curriculum and Instruction*, unpublished manuscript, pp. 6-33.

(8)

Category Four: Toward More Effective Behavior

The operational guides in Category Four offer practical suggestions for creative survival within an educational bureaucracy.

As the reader thinks about the guides presented in this chapter, he should recognize that bureaucracies by virtue of their emphasis on legal-rational systems are vulnerable to those who can be as legal and as rational—or more so—than their bureaucratic superiors. For example, bureaucracies typically have so many rules and regulations that they must obviously conflict one with another. Thus, the individual who knows his particular work responsibility well and who knows well those rules and regulations applying specifically to it, may often be the actor rather than the reactor in relationships with bureaucratic superiors.

This chapter is directed to those in the educational bureaucracy who have the courage of their convictions about what they want to do; who have carefully studied the organization and know what is actually prohibited and what is not; and who recognize the vulnerability of the bureaucratic structure to challenge those assumptions on which its legal-rational pronouncements rest.

Operational Guide 9

If you want to slow down change, make it visible.

We stated in Part 2 that there is from moment to moment in human relationships an actor and a reactor, and the main advantage of the actor role is greater control over the variables of the situation. The element of surprise is also an important consideration in the actor role; the reactor spends a great deal of time and energy in reacting to offensive moves by the actor. Therefore, if you want to slow down change, make it visible, for one thing that visibility does is clearly bring into focus for the benefit of the reactors exactly what you have done, are doing, and probably will do in the immediate future. It is also true that change is often threatening to those who are aware of it, and the more visible change is, the more threatening it is.

The educational decision-maker can benefit from couching the language of change in the language of the status quo, as far as this is possible. The decision-maker who feels it is necessary to put new labels on everything he does or wants to do only raises the anxiety level of those he hopes to engage in the change process. For example, a school system decided to introduce a "new" reading program, which in fact was more similar to than dissimilar from the previous reading program. Administrators and teachers in the school system made the mistake of introducing a whole new vocabulary to describe the "new" reading system, with the result that parents and their children reacted against the change.

The educational decision-maker who who wants to introduce a new program should emphasize its similarities to the program that parents and others are acquainted with, pointing out that differences are designed to improve rather than reject the status quo. The teacher who wants a more open school and more open classrooms need not talk about adopting the "open school" or the British primary school. Instead she should use more commonly understood terms such as individualized instruction, more freedom to the teachers, and greater opportunities for individual student development.

As far as possible, the stated objectives of the "status quo" should be used, for they are almost always broad enough to encompass any new program. One school system was particularly effective in introducing a new social studies program, emphasizing that the new program would meet existing goals and objectives by allowing for more flexible use of materials and student activities.

The teacher who wants to do something truly different should beware of challenging his colleagues, for a common reaction is that the innovator is implying that his way is better than that of his colleagues. Of course, one way to deal with this matter is to try to convert one's colleagues to the "new" way. A mathematics teacher had recently joined the staff of the local high school. She frequently spoke in the teachers' room about how well her students responded to the new approach to math instruction she had learned in summer school. She also pointed out how many of her students had said they wished their former teachers had taught that way. Her approach was in fact a frontal attack on her colleagues, and they did their best to isolate her from their activities.

One of the best ways to bring about instructional change is to proceed unobtrusively and carry it out in your own classroom. If the innovative approach is better, others will tend to see and adopt those parts of the change that work for them. A sixth grade teacher believed strongly in role playing and simulation experiences in the teaching of social studies. He asked some of his colleagues to visit his classroom and evaluate what happened. He particularly asked for suggestions that would improve his instructional approach. After a brief period of time it was apparent that a number of his colleagues were using role playing and simulation in their teaching.

For change to become institutionalized rather than a passing fad, those who carry it out must be committed to the change. They must see the change as meeting their needs, which means that it helps them do their job better. One principal who saw his teachers as bureaucrats hired to carry out his orders made a decree about team teaching: "This is the direction education is going and I've arranged teaching schedules as follows in order to get team teaching in the school." Those who had to live with the change on a day-to-day basis gave lip service to team teaching but did little more since they had no part in the decision and were not committed to it.

A principal in another school system worked closely with teachers in both the planning and implementation stages. Only those teachers who wanted to be involved in team teaching participated. Two years later more than 60 percent of the faculty were team teaching and the other 40 percent showed no interest in sabotaging the experiment. The second principal acted in a manner consistent with the professional rather than the bureaucratic model.

In recent years we have observed a phenomenon that seems to run counter to the postulate, "If you want to slow down change, make it visible." Leadership in the "Beat-Hippie-Yippie" movement[1] has depended on the mass media, especially television, to reach the minds and the feelings of our country's population. Because this movement has not had access to normal communication channels within "the establishment," it has instead depended on journalists, newsmen, and the like to draw attention to its beliefs. The leaders have had a good deal of success in "blowing the minds" of many in the establishment and in the process have received some following among those who are also disenchanted with the status quo.

At first glance it would appear as if such youth movements do not accept the objectives of the establishment, especially since they have invented their own language, which sounds foreign to those not acquainted with it. However, we find the same principles of governance and leadership-followership at work within these movements and organizations: leaders depend on their charisma for compliance; leaders play an interventionist role in minimizing controversy; a follower's value is determined by his contribution to the group; and a follower's proximity to the leader is very important both to his self-concept and to his ability to influence the power structure of the group.[2] We also find that leaders in these groups pay a good deal of attention to strategies for influencing events and individuals and organizations outside themselves. The layman who watches their antics on television or reads about them in the newspaper often has the impression that a bunch of "crazies are freaked out on drugs or whatever with each of them doing his own thing." In fact, leaders of these movements employ very deliberate political strategies in order to reach their goals.[3]

In summary, we must make a distinction between decision-making principles of an intergroup and intragroup variety, and we must also keep in mind the distinction between actor and reactor roles. Each role has its own strategies and tactics that explain in large measure the actions of those who play such roles.

Operational Guide 10

Although bureaucracies demand obedience to written rules and directives from "superiors," recognize that if something is not prohibited you can do it, and if it is prescribed you can do more.

If you as an educational decision-maker show obedience to written rules and regulations, you tend to generate trust on the part of bureaucratic superiors and colleagues, making it more likely that your deviations from many other established practices will be accepted. A middle-school teacher explained her support for this position as follows: "The administration, especially the principal's secretary, goes crazy when you don't have forms filled out and in on time. Although I don't like to spend time on these forms, I've discovered that filling them out and getting them in on time keeps from drawing attention to myself. This means that I can do other things that are kind of far out, but if I didn't take care of the forms the administration would be all over me for other things I do in my classroom." The teacher withstood a minor annoyance to achieve what she thought was a greater good. She did not believe in rebellion for its own sake, and she did not feel a need to demonstrate her independence from authority by fighting this particular aspect of being a teacher.

If you, the educational decision-maker, are departing from the norm, avoid the messianic syndrome. You don't need to tell everyone what you are doing and why it is different from and better than what they are presently doing. The teacher who feels compelled to tell everyone how superior is what she does in her teaching is by implication telling others that what they do is not good, that they are not able teachers.

This part of the postulate, "If something you want to do is not specifically prohibited, you can probably do it," is often overlooked by educational decision-makers. It should be added that you shouldn't ask your superior if you can do something that is not specifically prohibited, for his knowledge places some responsibility on him for what happens. Instead, do what is not prohibited and have a reasonable rationale for it. Too many teachers assume that they may only do what is already being done. Although this is the "safe" position, it is hardly creative and students will be the losers.

Bureaucracies, in this case schools, prescribe certain practices. The student teacher might be upset that she has to "cover" the American Revolution and the Constitutional Convention. The way in which the American Revolution and the Constitutional Convention are covered is rarely prescribed, so that many options are available to the student teacher. One student teacher, for example, compared the American, French, and Bolshevik revolutions. A second teacher covered the Constitutional Convention and challenged the students to build a case for the need for a new Constitutional Convention, after which they conducted a mock convention in the classroom. A common occurrence is for a teacher to use the statement, "We have to do this or that," as a crutch for not being innovative.

Operational Guide 11

Recognize that there are some students that you will not reach, others you will reach minimally, and still others for whom you will make an important difference in their lives.

The dean of a well-known medical school made these comments about patients who contact doctors: "Eighty percent will probably get well anyway unless you do something wrong, 10 percent are probably doomed, and there is another 10 percent for whom treatment is critical." Although the medical school dean's statement seems to be cold and analytical, a second reflection indicates that he is probably right although the percentages may vary from one person's projection to another. We might rephrase the statement so that it becomes a principle of value to the educational decision-maker: "You will make a significant difference in the lives of some of your students, you will make absolutely no difference in the lives of some of your students, and most of your students will not be affected very much one way or the other as a result of their contact with you."

One reaction to this operational guide runs counter to much of the idealistic rhetoric that surrounds teaching. As educators we have been taught that we will make a significant difference in the lives of all of our students. This kind of educational messianism is often every bit as strong as the evangelism of more formal, organized religions. The promise of such rhetoric sounds hollow to the first year teacher when he or she realizes that it simply isn't so once on the firing line.

What does this guide mean in specific terms for the educational decision-maker? It doesn't mean that you throw up your hands in frustration thinking that it is an all-or-none situation—that you reach all of them or none of them. It *does* mean that you recognize the realities of human relationships. It is very difficult for a teacher to know all her students well, or let us say it is certainly true that a teacher knows her students to varying degrees. Even for the teacher who knows her students reasonably well, she cannot have the knowledge and skills to optimally meet the needs of all. What she can do is avoid excessive guilt and the projection of that guilt onto her students whereby it becomes "their fault."

Thus far we have indicated that the teacher can't control all of the variables to the extent of being a significant influence on the lives of all of his students. This leads us to the matter of sources of power of the control the educational decision-maker, in this case the teacher, exercises over students. The first source of power is *positional authority*. Mr. Brown believes that his formal position as a teacher gives him the power to do what he feels students need to do. This source of power was once quite effective in the schools, for children were taught to obey their parents, teachers, and other authority figures. For a variety of reasons, this source of power has become less and less viable for the teacher. A less structured atmosphere in families and the breakdown of many families, plus the knowledge explosion as evidenced by the availability of television programming, have lessened the influence of positional authority.

A second source of power is *expertise*. Mrs. White knows her students quite well and most of them recognize that her knowledge and teaching skills clearly qualify her as an expert teacher. Her discipline problems are few although many of her colleagues feel that she fails to keep the proper social distance from her students. At the same time it is recognized that she has an advanced degree from a prestigious university and has twice won the Teacher of the Year award.

Charisma is a third source of power for the teacher. This source is especially powerful at the early elementary school level. Miss Black is well liked by all her pupils and they want to please her. She rewards them with affection and approval and they probably think she is more beautiful and younger than mommy even if she isn't. In our judgment, charisma has become a much more important source of power as valued by students. One of the reasons for this is the importance of charisma in the nonschool lives of students. Television is a major source of this influence.

The challenge to the teacher as an educational decision-maker is to find ways to reach a larger percentage of students. The extent to which a decision is accepted by a group is a function of the degree to which they participate in making it. This is not to say, however, that the quality of a decision—its validity—is necessarily related to the number of people who participate in making it. For example, a fifth grade student brought a muskrat to class for "show-and-tell" time. A classmate asked whether the animal was male or female. Since no one in the room knew the answer to this question, they decided to vote on it. Obviously, their vote was less valid than the opinion of a zoologist. Likewise, the fact that students are involved for two or three weeks in planning something does not necessarily mean that such planning is more valid than the teacher's plan that was made in less than half a day. Nevertheless, it remains true that the degree to which a group participates in the formation of a decision affects the extent to which they will accept the decision. Therefore the "mythical 80 percent" cited by the medical school dean will probably give more support to educational decisions which they have had a part in forming.

To influence a person to do something, you have him perceive what you want him to do as meeting one or more needs that are important to him, or you prevent him from meeting a need that he now is able to meet. The former is a much more positive approach, while the latter is the poorest form of motivation because the person is coerced and will only do enough to have the threat removed. For example, Johnny needs to feel accepted by his classmates. The more positive approach is to find activities that can help him achieve acceptance; the more negative approach is to threaten him with punishments so that he will conform only while he perceives the threat to exist.

As we indicated earlier, the most significant changes in students' lives are often brought about by teachers through affective (feeling) learning. A kind of self-fulfilling prophecy takes place, for the student tends to behave according to the positive image of him that the teacher and fellow students project. That is, his self-image or self-concept is manipulated in a positive direction. One teacher expressed this belief in the following manner: "Every student here can excel at something worthwhile, and my job is to find out what it is and provide him with the opportunity to excel at it."

Case Study 1

Mary Claxton was beginning her first day of teaching at Westwood School. She had been invited by another teacher, George Allen, to join him at coffee in the teacher's lounge after the orientation meeting for new teachers. George poured her a cup of coffee, handed it to her, and the two of them took seats in the corner of the lounge away from a rather loud and hilarious group gathered around the conference table in the lounge.

Mary had known George for about ten years. He had been a close friend of her family, and he and her father were about the same age. George had taught at Westwood for almost nine years, and before that had taught in another school in the system for ten years. George began, "Mary, I just though I might give you a few hints about how to get along at Westwood. Mike Allen, the principal, runs a tight ship. Make sure all of your reports are in on time. Make sure that your classroom is always neat and orderly. And, for goodness sake, make sure that your students do well on standardized tests. Mike likes to think of himself as a real 'democratic leader,' but what he means when he says that is that he wants you to express your opinion, but it should conform with his. I know you've learned many interesting techniques in college, and probably some of them would work somewhere. But here, if you stick to the basic skills and keep the kids in line—and I mean keep them in line—you'll be happier, the kids'll be happier, and you'll be a good successful teacher."

"But, Mr. Allen," Mary said, "When I had my interview with the principal, he seemed most receptive when I told him about some of the things I wanted to do. In fact, he said one of the requisites he had for any new teacher was that the teacher be imaginative, innovative, and really do what she thought was a good job. He said that he sees his role as adviser, that he considers his teachers professional people, and fully believes that the final decisions as far as instruction is concerned should be left to them."

"Well, I'm sure that's what he said, and he'll say it again if he can, but take my word for it, don't you believe it."

Case Study 2

Mr. Watts, the principal at Donnely School, began the third faculty meeting of the year by saying, "I am pleased to announce that all of our teachers, with the exception of one, have joined the Teacher's Professional Association for this school year. Donnely School has always had 100 percent membership in the professional association. Perhaps I have not made it clear in the past how important that is. Let me now emphasize that I feel it is exceedingly important for professionals to maintain membership in their professional organization. Now, Mr. Watson, I'm sure you have good reason for not having joined up to this point, but I would appreciate it if you would share with the group what your reasons are. Would you please do so now?"

Bill Watson looked at Mr. Watts, looked around the room, cleared his throat, and said . . . .

Case Study 3

Mark Shapiro, the assistant principal of Carver Junior High School, returned to his office to find every chair and every available inch of sitting room on the floor occupied by a delegation of students. Jack Burns, apparently the leader of the group, and a boy whom Mark knew to be quite influential among the students in the school, greeted him with the statement, "Shapiro, we've taken about all we can take. We've been pushed around too long. We're marched from class to class. We're treated as if we are in prison. You have armed guards roaming the hallway, the doors are padlocked, and once we get into school the teachers line us up and search us. We're treated like criminals—maybe it's time we started acting like criminals. We've decided that beginning tomorrow we get treated like human beings. Or else, if you think you've seen trouble, you ain't seen nothing."

The group burst into applause, and there were various remarks from several of them: "You tell 'im, man." "You dig that, Shapiro?" "We'll sit here till the end of time, man, till the end of time unless we get some satisfaction, you dig it, man, you dig it."

Shapiro made a few remarks to the group designed primarily to calm them down a bit and let them know he had gotten the message, then asked if they would leave now and send some representatives tomorrow to talk to him after he'd had a chance to check into what all of the problems bothering them were. After perhaps twenty minutes of rather heated exchange, the group agreed and left. Shaprio sat down at his desk and reread the directive that had just come from the central office:

To: All principals
From: Superintendent A.J. Spires
Subject: Discipline within the schools

Following a Board resolution expressing profound concern with the lack of discipline within our junior high schools and high schools, I have been directed by the Board to implement the following policies:

1. Increase security in all schools by employing one security guard for every 800 students in each junior and senior high school in the city.
2. Meet any act of defiance on the part of the student with immediate action that will result in the suspension or expulsion of the student.
3. Establish written codes of behavior for all students to be enforced by teachers with the full backing of the administration of each school.
4. Allow no disruption of the education process by any student.

Each principal will be held fully responsible for implementing the above policies.

If you have any questions or suggestions as to the implementation of these policies, please contact my office.

At the bottom of the memo was scrawled: "Implement these, Mark, and let me know what you've done and when they can all be fully implemented. [Signed] J.B."

Mark thought, "Well, that's typical of J.B. He learned in his course in administration if you're the principal, delegate the tough task to the assistant principal."

Case Study 4

John Jarrett, assistant dean of Arts and Sciences, reread the memo he had just received from Dean of Students Dan Thomas. The memo concerned a student with whom Jarrett had been working closely and recommended that disciplinary charges be brought against the student. Thomas contended in his memo that, "Will Smith was a bad influence on other students since he used violent and abusive language in the student center, and since the uncouthness of his language was fully matched by the uncouthness of his dress and his body hygiene." Thomas recommended that Smith be brought before the University Discipline Committee and charged with conduct unbecoming a student at the university.

Dean Jarrett knew that Smith had more than his share of emotional problems and was, in fact, in therapy with a local psychiatrist. Smith's academic record was well above average: he had, during his three years' attendance at the university, maintained a B plus average. Though several professors had complained about his attitude in class, stating that he was quite argumentative, almost to the point of disrupting class activities, none had anything but praise for his academic abilities and performance.

As Dean Jarrett pondered the memo and the circumstances which led to it, he was concerned that if Smith were called before a disciplinary committee he would very quickly, concisely, and directly point out what he thought of disciplinary committees in general, and more to the point, what he thought of the one that dared charge him. It was now Monday, and the disciplinary committee was to meet on Friday.

Case Study 5

Dean Jarrett was most impressed by the arguments put forth by the student with whom he was talking. Mack Jones was a first semester junior, intensely articulate with a spotty academic record—As and Ds. For the last forty minutes he had been describing to Dean Jarrett his plans to become a writer and had very rationally pointed out why the degree requirements at the university did not provide him with an educational experience that was currently meaningful or relevant to his future plans.

Jarrett knew that Jones had exceptional talent as a writer. He had published widely in local university publications and had two articles accepted by a national magazine, so his talk about becoming a writer was more than wishful thinking.

Jarrett was still not clear about just what it was Jones wanted, so he asked, "Mack, just what is it you want to do?"

Jones replied, "I want to select the courses and professors that seem most appropriate to me and accumulate my 122 hours in that manner rather than the manner that the university has prescribed, primarily because I think I am a much better judge of what is a sound education for me than are a group of professors who claim to be able to teach me to write but who are incapable of writing an article worthy of publication in anything but the most esoteric journals. All I want from you, Dean Jarrett, is a straight answer. Can I do that?"

Case Study 6

Two weeks had gone by following the faculty retreat held to develop some preliminary plans for the new undergraduate curriculum for the School of Education at the university. Bill Rogers, associate dean of the School of Education, had been charged with the responsibility for planning and, in turn, chairing the retreat by the dean of the school. The retreat had gone well for the first two days; not too many concrete proposals had been made, but the twelve faculty participating had begun to exchange information in a less defensive manner than had been the case when the retreat started. A few modest proposals had come forth, but they deviated little from the current practices in the school, and Rogers knew they certainly would not be the kinds of proposals the dean had expected the retreat to produce.

On the evening of the third day of the retreat, the dean met with the group for dinner, which was preceded by more than a few cocktails. During the dinner the dean chastised two of the senior faculty members for their failure to show imagination and leadership. When the group reconvened after dinner, the dean spoke for about thirty minutes and indicated to the group that he had expected, and still expected, some imaginative and innovative proposals from them. He then left.

For perhaps five minutes after the dean's departure there was silence. Then one of the senior professors who had been dressed down by the dean at dinner spoke: "Since I am one who was singled out as not doing the job we were sent here to do, I feel that I need to make a few remarks which I hope you will not think I am making to defend myself. First, let me say that I have great respect for the dean and have been a close personal friend of his for the past ten years. I saw, as did all of you, that he is quite agitated at this time, and I think for good reason. He is, as some of you may know, under tremendous pressure from the central administration to secure funds for a new school of education building and to secure some support for research and development of new undergraduate curricula. Perhaps his expectations of us are unrealistic, but I do believe that we should, for the remaining day of this retreat, try to come up with something reasonably sound and specific."

The group worked until two in the morning and for another six hours the following day, drawing up a proposal for a new undergraduate program in teacher education.

Charged by the dean with the task of drafting the curriculum proposal, and with implementing it once it was approved, following the retreat Rogers called two meetings of the faculty who had participated in the retreat. In Rogers' judgment, these meetings had been less than fruitful since the members of the group had spent most of their time discussing whether six hours of English or nine hours of English should be required, whether educational psychology should precede student teaching or be taught concurrently with it, and similar issues that indicated to him that the faculty was dealing with the new proposal as if it were just one of a number of old curriculum issues to be solved in the same way: change a course title or a course number, add a course or change course sequences.

As Rogers again read the rough draft of the new curriculum proposal, the phone rang. Dean Shoals was on the line. "Bill," he said, "do you think that the new curriculum proposal will be in shape so that we can take it before the general faculty of education in two weeks? You know that the Ipswich Foundation is waiting for a proposal from us, and if we get it in within the next month, they are likely to give us favorable consideration this year. I have good reason to believe that they will underwrite the primary instructional costs for the first three years. Assuming that those three years are successful, I believe that we can go back to them for a major grant for a school of education building. I don't expect you to give me a definite answer at this moment, but could you within a day or two tell me what you think the chances are?"

After the usual amenities and friendly chitchat, Rogers said goodbye and hung up the phone and looked again at the rough draft of the proposal. In his judgment the faculty who had worked on it were neither committed to it nor particularly in agreement with it. The group was to meet again that afternoon and Rogers knew that some critical decisions would have to be made about the current proposal. He had two hours before the meeting to decide on what strategies he might employ.

Case Study 7

Bart Masters, vice-president of academic affairs at the university, invited Professor Post into his office. Post had requested an appointment with Masters to discuss his reemployment for the following academic year. Professor Post had had a long career with the university, having served as chairman of the Department of History for fifteen years prior to reaching the retirement age of sixty-five. For the past two years he had been employed full time in the History Department on a year-to-year basis, since board policy did not permit anyone to hold an administrative post after age sixty-five, nor did it permit professors to be continued after that age except on a year-to-year contractual agreement. Masters had known Post for twelve years. They had served as fellow chairmen when Masters was chairman of the English Department and Post chairman of the History Department. When Masters became dean of Arts and Sciences he had valued Post as one of his most effective departmental chairmen.

Professor Post began by saying, "Bart, I always feel that this ritual is somewhat demeaning, but I assume it's necessary for both of us to put ourselves through it. This conversation is to give you official notice that I would like to continue in my present position as professor of history here for the next academic year. As you know, I am in no position to retire at this time, since my youngest child is still in high school and I still have two youngsters in college. I believe that I am capable of doing as effective a teaching job as I was able to do ten years ago, so that I don't believe that I am a charity case. I think the university receives full value for the salary it pays me."

Masters replied, "Frank, I know that you are one of our most effective professors. You certainly have given long and faithful service, and I am sure that the university will give every consideration to your request. I need to point out to you, however, that the Board of Trustees has expressed concern about the number of people we are keeping on beyond the age of sixty-five. Most members of the Board feel that our pension plan is a good one, that faculty over sixty-five are receiving maximum salary, and that retaining a number of faculty who have reached retirement age tends to clog up the upper ranks and possibly serve to discourage some of our younger faculty members. Also, to be quite candid, I believe that some of the trustees feel that we could replace several of our senior faculty with younger men who might do just as good a job and for significantly less salary. I am not telling you this is to be unduly pessimistic, but just to put your request in a realistic framework. As you know, President Johnson has been asked by the Board of Trustees to review our retirement policy and to make recommendations to them before the end of this academic year."

Post responded, "Bart, I realize the problems that you face, and again I am sorry for burdening you with my personal problems. However, let me reiterate that I do need to continue my employment if at all possible and I assure you that the university will receive services from me commensurate with their investment."

After Post left, Masters looked through the report that he was preparing for President Johnson on the current status of faculty over sixty-five who were being retained on a year-to-year basis. Out of a faculty of 600 there were fifteen such members who had been employed for the current academic year. Thirteen had requested reemployment for the following year; of those thirteen, only one could be considered irreplaceable. He was a distinguished professor of literature with a national reputation who headed the Great Books Symposium, which had brought recognition to the university from scholars throughout the region.

Masters knew that President Johnson, unlike his predecessor President Jones, did not favor retaining faculty beyond the age of sixty-five except in exceptional circumstances. Johnson believed that although some older faculty might well make substantial contributions to the university, those contributions could probably be duplicated by younger men. Masters reread the board policy statement on retention of faculty beyond age sixty-five: "In exceptional cases, faculty may be retained beyond the retirement age of sixty-five years. Such cases, however, should be documented by the president of the university, and such documentation should indicate that the professor is in good health and cannot at this time be replaced by someone of comparable ability and potential for contribution to the university."

Masters knew that Post's health was not good. In fact, he had missed more than six weeks of school during the past year; and though Masters was not certain of the facts, he understood that Post might well need to undergo surgery during the next academic year. While Post was an able teacher, he was not distinguished, either as a teacher or researcher. He had served the university faithfully and well for more than thirty years, and Masters had grown to respect his integrity, his intellect, and his dedication to the university. Masters knew that Post had some serious personal financial problems, since his wife was unable to work because of a heart condition and his three children were still in school.

Masters personally wanted to retain Post, but he was concerned about how this retention would affect the retention of the other professors who had requested continued employment. He was also concerned with President Johnson's reaction and with the reaction of the board, were he to request that Post be retained.

Case Study 8

Dean of Students Tom Watson listened as Mack Burnes, president of the Student Government Association at the university, recounted some of the conversation that had taken place that morning at a meeting of the executive committee of the SGA. Burnes was worried that a confrontation might take place the following morning when the flag was raised. He was certain that his information was reasonably correct that some groups of students were likely to try to prevent the flag from being raised, while another group intended to appear at the flagpole to make certain that the flag was raised.

Watson went on, "As you know, Dean, quite a number of our students are very upset by the deaths of two students at ______ College in Louisiana, and feel very strongly that at least a day of mourning here would be appropriate. They definitely intend to lower the flag to half-mast in the morning as a symbol of our concern for the events in Louisiana. Another group which seemed to me like a bunch of super-patriots contend that the students killed were breaking the law and the flag certainly should not be lowered to honor criminals who were shot in the act of committing a crime. I think the whole thing seems rather silly to make such a to-do over whether or not the flag is raised, but tempers are running high and I thought you ought to know."

"Now, when is all this supposed to occur?" Watson asked.

"Tomorrow at 8:00 when the flag is raised—or supposed to be raised."

Watson knew Burnes to be a very reliable person, and on many occasions information from Burnes had helped prevent what might have otherwise have been serious incidents on the campus. It was now 3:30 in the afternoon, and Watson knew that before 8:00 tomorrow morning he would need a well-conceived course of action. He was particularly concerned that the president of the university, Dr. Smyth, not be unduly alarmed since Smyth had a tendency to overreact when he felt the authority of the university was being challenged, and particularly when that challenge might also have political repercussions.

Case Study 9

John Joyner was a first year principal. As a former teacher in the school John had occasionally used corporal punishment as stipulated by school policy: the student had always been swatted on the bottom in the presence of an administrator. As a principal John intended to continue this same policy.

On a Thursday morning in April the father of a child who had been punished on Wednesday came into the principal's office. His demeanor was that of a concerned and somewhat angry parent. He was very articulate. "I'm not very happy about my son being swatted but I'm even unhappier about corporal punishment being used in this day and age in our school. One of the things you teach children when you hit them is that they should hit other children when they do something wrong."

John had not heard this argument before, and he paused before answering. "I think children know it's the adult's role to swat children when they deserve it. Kids know this doesn't mean they can hit other kids."

"Some children may make this role distinction but others will not," said the parent. "I get all the school literature on individualized learning and teaching, and yet you don't even know the difference between those who know the role distinction and those who don't—or at least you swat both groups."

John paused again, not sure what to say. He also wondered in his own mind how teachers would react to a change in disciplinary policy.

Case Study 10

Walt Bonds was in his second year as a social studies teacher at Miller High School. Miller High School was located in a midwestern city, population approximately 160,000, and had recently been integrated by court order. Prior to court-ordered integration, Miller High School had had approximately 96 percent white students and 4 percent black students. When the city was ordered to close Grant High School, which had been more than 90 percent black, Miller received a large number of the Grant pupils, and the school population became approximately 58 percent white and 42 percent black.

Walt believed that social studies instruction in high school should be a great deal more than the teaching of history or government or of the technical skills and concepts of the social sciences. He believed that social studies, to perform the proper service for high school students, should cause them to think about themselves and their relationship to others, and even more to feel about themselves and relationships to others in a way that would promote better understanding, and thus better relationships among individuals of all races and creeds. He often employed role-playing activities and simulations designed to duplicate actual situations of human stress brought about by racial tensions. He felt that the greatest service he might perform as a social studies teacher at this time was to help blacks and whites in his classes get to know each other better, understand each other, and relate to each other as human beings rather than as members of one race to members of another race.

For the past month Walt had had members of his class play various roles in class exercises designed to promote the understanding and acceptance he believed was so important.

It was now Friday afternoon, and Walt was rather pleased with how the activities had been going. In fact, he was certain that he saw much less tension than he had seen at the beginning of the year. As he was preparing to leave his classroom, Tom Ellington, the principal, walked in and said, "Walt, do you have a few minutes? I'd like to ask a few questions."

Walt said, "Fine, Tom, go ahead."

"Walt, I've been hearing about some of the activities you've been doing with your students. They sound quite interesting, but I do have a few questions about them. First of all, are you sure that you're actually covering American history when you have people play roles about human relations involving blacks and whites? Now, don't get me wrong. I know what your purposes are, and I fully agree with them. But you *are* supposed to be covering American history in this class, and I wonder if you're able to do so. Further, are you sure you're qualified to deal with such volatile issues? After all, having these people get together and talk about their problems may help, but it may also blow up in our faces. You know I have a great deal of faith in you as a teacher, and I'd be the last to tell you not to do something. But I wonder if you might not take a more normal approach to your teaching and at least for the next few weeks get back to the business of teaching American history. What do you think about that, Walt?"

Case Study 11

Bill Watkins, a guidance counselor at Perkins High School, sat down at his desk and began to read a memorandum from the school principal, John Weldon. The memo concerned the use and sale of drugs by students at Perkins High School, and read:

To: Administrative and guidance staff
From: John Weldon, Principal
Subject: Drug use and sale by students at Perkins High School

This memo is to be treated in the strictest confidence. I am concerned about the increased use of drugs and even more concerned about the fact that some of them might well be sold on campus. I expect soon, with the help of the police, to institute a thorough search of the school, and also to provide an effective intelligence network so that we can learn very quickly if drugs are brought to school and by whom they are brought. Obviously I need the full cooperation of the administrative and guidance staff.

If any of you hear of a student who has drugs, or of a student who knows about someone else possessing drugs, I want you to notify me immediately, giving me all the details you have. I can then proceed to take proper action, either as principal of the school, or I can ask for police assistance.

Your cooperation in this matter is essential.

As Watkins finished reading the memo, his secretary buzzed him and told him that Sam Dodson, a student, wanted to see him as soon as possible. Watkins told her to send Sam in.

Sam, a husky six-footer and a star on the high school baseball team, entered and shook hands with Bill. Bill could tell that Sam was most upset. He asked him to take a seat, but Sam said, "No, I think I'd rather stand for what I have to say I can say very quickly. And I'm just too uncomfortable to sit down." He went on, "Mr. Watkins, what I'm going to tell you I hope you will keep confidential. I don't want to get anybody in any trouble. All I want to do is help. I probably shouldn't be here, and I know that if any of the guys know I am here I'm really in for it. But I think you should know what's bothering me, and I think you're the person I want to talk to because I trust you and I know you will use what I am telling you in a way that nobody is going to get hurt. There are at least six or seven boys on the baseball team who are using uppers and downers and I don't know what else. I know they often have whites, reds, and blues. A lot of times they may take one or two before a game, and usually after a game when we go out to celebrate they take two or three or four. I'm not going to tell you who they are, and I don't think anybody could make me tell, but I wanted you to know about it, and I guess I've said all I should say."

Watkins replied, "Sam, don't you think you might give me a few more details? Or at least give me some suggestions about what you think I might do. Why don't you sit down and let's talk about this in somewhat more detail?"

"No, Mr. Watkins, I can't tell you any more. I'm going to be late for class. I'll see you later. 'Bye." And Sam went out the door.

Watkins knew that Sam was a very dependable young man, highly respected by his fellow students, and by teachers. He wished that Sam had given him more information, but he did not feel that in any way he should press the boy to give any more. He glanced again at the principal's memo, and mumbled to himself, "Well, Bill, now let's call into play all of those things you learned in graduate school."

Notes for Chapter 8

1. The incredible rate of speed at which these movements emerge and disappear makes any kind of accurate labelling dysfunctional, but we refer at large to the movement that started with Jack Kerouac and went through a series of others like Ken Kesey and Abbie Hoffman.

2. See for example Tom Wolfe's *The Electric Kool-Aid Acid Test* (New York: Bantam Books, 1968), pp. 142, 144, 240.

3. Ken Kesey's Pranksters, for example, sometimes operated on the principle, "If you're too obvious, you won't be seen." This was reflected in their dress, transportation, and the like. Wolfe, *The Electric Kool-Aid Acid Test,* p. 181.

Epilogue

The usual purpose of an epilogue is to complete the plan for the authors' work, and yet we feel we have hardly begun our study of educational organizations. We view the conclusion of this book as a brief pause in our inquiry into and dialogue about educational organizations. As such our epilogue is both encouragement and challenge to the reader and to ourselves.

The ideas set forth in *Decision-Making in Educational Organizations* were the result of our interaction with others in organizations in general, and educational organizations in particular. The obvious challenge is to involve one's self in educational praxis or reflective action in order to try out the ideas discussed in the book.

We are especially interested in seeing what happens when particular educational organizations implement the organizational model we have proposed in chapter 3. This model advocates a marriage of bureaucratic and professional organizational models within a single educational organization. The bureaucratic aspect is designed to implement governance functions, and the professional aspect focuses on curriculum and instruction matters.

We began our discussion in this book by describing decision-making as the process by which a basic dilemma is resolved: People have unlimited desires but limited resources. There is no one right way to allocate and organize resources in order to implement the bureaucratic-professional model we have advocated. Educators interested in implementing this model will need to assess their own organization's strengths, weaknesses, and potentialities before adopting strategies for initiating and maintaining the bureaucratic-professional model. We are presently engaged in this process ourselves and hope in the near future to continue our dialogue on educational organizations.

We have seen enough positive results from applying ideas from this book to decision-making situations to warrant encouragement and optimism. It is our hope that the reader will become engaged in implementing the book's ideas and feel likewise.

Index